RESIDUAL
life

How To Build A
Network Marketing
Empire

MICHELLE SCHAFFER

**Energy4PR
Publishers**
"your story;
their hope"

Paperback ISBN: 978-1-64570-475-1
Digital ISBN: 978-1-64570-474-4
The Residual Life:
How To Build A Network Marketing Empire
www.michelleschaffer.com

Connect on Instagram @ teenmomtomillionaire
Follow Michelle's Podcast: *The Souled-Out Entrepreneur*

Table of Contents

" The Lord will open the heavens, the storehouse of his bounty, to send rain on your land in season and to bless all the work of your hands. You will lend to many nations but will borrow from none. "

- Deut 28:12 NIV

" Anyone looking to jumpstart their success in Network Marketing will benefit from this book. Michelle's vast personal experience provides invaluable lessons that will save you time and propel you towards your financial goals. "

- Travis Ogden, CEO, Isagenix

" Michelle's an expert at Network Marketing. Her passion for this profession is loud and clear. She's been in Network Marketing for 15 years and has achieved phenomenal success. In this book, she will give you proven tips to build your business, from her experience in building 3 separate business's from scratch. The new way of Network Marketing has evolved, and she has a clear path to accelerate your success. A must read for anyone serious about this profession. "

- Kathy Coover, Co-Founder, Isagenix Int'l

" Michelle's one of those rare network marketers that can perform the necessary skills with discipline that it takes to be successful; and, she can also mentor and train others in her no-nonsense way to do the same. She's one of the most positive, energetic masters in the Network Marketing industry with no fail systems and processes that stand the test of time. "

- Kristina Swift, VP of Sales, Plexus

" Want to save years of learning curves, investing your energy instead into building a lasting legacy with residual income and timeless ripple effect? Read *The Residual Life*! Michelle highlights the tried and tested principles that help entrepreneurs elevate and steward the noble profession of Network Marketing! "

- Tim Hooper, Speaker & Author, *GotEnergy?*

Dedication

This book is dedicated to the dreamers, the visionaries and the ones who will never settle. I also want to dedicate this book to my mentor Bobby Schaffer. You have poured into me your passion for this profession, your knowledge of it and your love for people. You have led the way for me, patiently teaching me all you know. You have shown me how I needed to grow in the most loving ways. I am so grateful for all you've taught me. And lastly, this book is dedicated to my three children. It is because of you that I stepped out into the unknown. I pray each of you have the courage to follow your hearts and create lives that you love.

Foreword

HEY SLOW DOWN ... Don't flip the page until you read this foreword! "Why?", you may ask ... Because I want to share with you some insights into Michelle and what you will soon learn about her and how to transform your legacy moving forward.

What you have in your hands, isn't just the epic adventure of a beautiful, successful, and articulate woman. This book is truly a historical journey that you can use to collapse the timeframe in your own Network Marketing adventure.

You will learn the art and science behind how a tattered princess, who was looking for her own knight in shining armor, realized what she truly needed and climbed out of her own emotional disheartening fairytale to grow into a Proverbs 31 woman.

WAIT RIGHT THERE Mr. STUD ... just about ready to close the book? This is also for YOU! If you bought or picked this book up, the odds are your business has either plateaued, or you're looking for answers on how to help your team duplicate the same success you've enjoyed. As a matter of fact, you may be thinking, "I have team members who see me as a knight in shining armor," and yet you feel like a tarnished knight, not having a clue how to help them. Michelle's story and what she shares will help you sir!

Michelle, may be the first person to take you into an area of Network Marketing, known only to the ultimate successful. You will learn some valuable, private and until now, well-guarded secrets, known by many, and practiced only by the top 10% of multipliers in the Network Marketing profession. This isn't information you will learn from those self-proclaimed, social media, MLM gurus. This is the exact blueprint Michelle and Bobby used to create the legacy for hundreds, if not thousands, who have trusted them with their financial futures.

One of the most valuable nuggets of wisdom you will gain from this book is how to develop and use your "Circle of Trust". This one nugget is worth the investment in this book.

You will learn the real meaning of W.I.T. and how, when used properly, this one strategy will collapse the timeframe it takes for you and your team to see financial and personal success.

Most of all, what you have here is a true book of wisdom. If you make this book part of your business strategy and get a copy in the hands of your team, and apply this information exactly as Michelle shares, then within 18 to 24 months, you will see some amazing things happen.

As a bonus to all who have read this far ... if, after reading and applying 100% of the wisdom you learn from Michelle, you believe this information is worthless, then contact me personally, and I will share with you how you can get 100% of your money back! This will not be from Michelle, but from me personally! Now there will be one catch ... no two:

1. You will have to agree to a 3-way call with both Michelle and I, sharing your experience and answering some very important questions.

2. I will want the book sent back to me, so I can get it into the hands of others.

Michelle, I'm so honored for the privilege of writing this foreword, and to be a small part of the transformation of so many. From a very young age you showed the Lord, He could trust you with much ... and you're still giving it away!

Living An Epic Adventure,
Troy Dooly
The Beachside CEO

Introduction

If you are new to Network Marketing, Direct Sales, Influencer Marketing, or Multi-Level Marketing, or if you have just a little experience or you are already a pro, this book is for you. If you are a total skeptic or a passionate lover of the profession, you are going to love this book! It will open your eyes and help you understand why so many people around the world have chosen it as a career and been so financially successful.

I have read almost every book written on the profession of Network Marketing. Many of them written a decade ago or longer, and many of them written from a Man's perspective. I decided it was time to write a book that tells it like it is in this crazy, wild, unexpected profession from my point of view.

I fell in love with it 15 years ago and boy oh boy I've seen a lot over the years. I have held many roles, both corporate and as a distributor. I have been consistent enough to be very successful. I have lots of battle scars. I have watched the profession shift, grow and change. I have worked with just about every type of person you could imagine. I've achieved a level of success that people dream of, and I have felt the pain of failure.

As I have walked this chosen road, I have been able to set

aside a whole lot of knowledge that I plan to pass on to you. I want to give it to you straight. I won't fluff it up. I will tell you the truth which can sometimes be ugly, and I will give you tools and actual steps you can take to reach the levels of success you've been dreaming about. I have built three separate Network Marketing businesses to six figure and multiple six figure incomes without having advantages or special treatments. My husband Bobby has built 5 Network Marketing businesses to six figures and multiple six figures a year. Together we have built businesses, taught and mentored others to create massive incomes and incredible success, and I can't wait for you to take this knowledge and apply it to your journey in this remarkable profession!

The Network Marketing world is not for the faint of heart. It takes a measure of entrepreneurship and emotional intelligence. It takes influence, leadership, and persistence. If you don't currently possess any of these traits, I will teach you how to grow and attain those very important characteristics. I will teach you the fundamentals of the business and explain to you how and why it works.

I will also give you an additional perspective. My mentor in this profession is someone who has over 30 years of experience. He has taught me everything I know, and he has different views on a lot of things. His knowledge is like gold and will add so much value to your training. I've included his knowledge over his long career in this book and put them in my own words for you.

You will get it ALL in the pages of this book. Grab a notebook, a highlighter and a pen. Mark this baby up. Allow it to serve as your guidebook for success and growth to build your own Residual Life.

Michelle

" Network Marketing isn't for the faint of heart "

What Is This?

Chapter 1

"If I would be given a chance to start all over again, I would choose network marketing." – Bill Gates

Network Marketers were one of the first great INFLUENCERS. They used their personal experience or testimonial with their product or service to influence the people in their circle to try them. Network Marketing, put very simply, is a method of product distribution. It is a highly efficient way for a product manufacturer to put their products directly into the hands of their customer/consumer without the use of a middleman, without spending millions on advertising and without having to hire a sales force to get the word out about their products. It's brilliant! With this distribution method, the customers ARE the sales force. Jubilant and satisfied customers sing the praises of their favorite products and get rewarded by the company for doing so.

This brilliant and 'peculiar' method began in 1886 with a company called The California Perfume Company. We would know this company today as Avon. David McConnell began as a bookseller. As a true entrepreneur, he realized the power of word of mouth marketing which allowed a person the opportunity to control their own destiny.

David McConnell wrote to his workforce in 1892:

> *"Dear Friends, We have decided to place these goods on the market after our own peculiar method, and will necessarily have to make confidants of a large number of worthy and enterprising people in order that we may carry out this system perfectly ..."*

As history shows, McConnell brought his perfumes direct to the customer through this"peculiar method" and his "New Industry" proved to be a phenomenal success.

In its infancy, it was a door to door selling model, and one that utilized the demonstration of products to the customers. This allowed the sales person to work as hard, or not, as they wanted too. This was a particularly exciting opportunity for women. This opened new doors for women to earn money at a time when those opportunities were not readily available. Over the years this evolved in exciting ways! What began as DIRECT SELLING or manufacturer direct to consumer, became multilevel marketing. This allowed the consumer sales person to find and train other consumer sales people, and earn from the sales created by them as well. They were being paid on multiple levels of a sales force that they themselves both recruited and trained. This was an exciting prospect for business owners. A company could then rely on the customers to bring more sales people, (Also customers) who also brought more sales people. The only cost to the company was the commission paid as products were sold. Again, **BRILLIANT!** This model is still an incredibly efficient and cost effective way to move products.

So let's get into it because I know what you're thinking right now. For those of you that haven't yet enrolled in a Network Marketing company, you are thinking PYRAMID. I get it. If I am being honest, it bugs me that this is STILL something people say. But I know that I need to address it and give you the truth once and for all so you will be armed with the CORRECT information. Where did this pyramid thing even start. Well, in the 70's, 80's and even the 90's the Network Marketing world was like a teenager. It was wild and rebellious. It made up its own rules. It loved the idea of fast money. It was immature and defiant. It snuck out of the house and stole the car, and it smoked and skipped school a lot. (Well, hopefully your teenagers aren't doing all of this haha!) The profession was trying desperately to figure out its identity. A company would launch with a sub-par product that people didn't really love, but had a compensation structure that allowed people to make lots of money. Many times it would be too much money, and the company would go out of business quickly. Crazy compensation plans that focused on paying the sales force for recruitment more than actual product sales became the norm. People would purchase products as a means to an end for getting paid, but not because they loved and used the products. Eventually, this unruly teen decided to omit products all together. In some cases, it became a flat out money and recruiting game. In the 80's one of these games was called 'airplanes.' People LOVED them! They basically were just money exchanging hands. All you had to do was bring in a few people with cash in hand. You didn't have to sell anything but just recruit a few people with some cash and get paid fast. Quite frankly it got out of hand. People got dollar signs in their eyes and many people LOST OUT! They didn't get a product, they had NOTHING! If they didn't go find a few other people the airplane crashed, and only the people who got in first or started it got paid. Companies with actual products would pay the sales field much more for recruiting people who purchased very expensive 'business starter packs' which was called front loading, that would sometimes cost in upwards of $5,000 or more. People would end up with so much product stacking up in their garage with not enough customers to sell it to, thus the old saying 'garage qualified'. And the illegal pyramid scheme was born.

But all was NOT lost! This wild teenager began to grow up a bit. The government finally began to create some guidelines and regulations to protect people from the scams. Direct Selling/Network Marketing/ MLM was made legal once and for all in a landmark court case in 1979 when Amway defeated the FTC.

The following is what the law recognizes as a legal company:

- No commissions for recruiting but only on the sale of products.

- Retail sales driven -- Representatives must retail the product.

- Inventory buy back -- The company must offer to purchase back unopened and unused inventory.

- 70% rule -- Representatives must consume or sell 70% of their inventory before ordering more.

So now that our teenager has grown up a bit, why do people still talk about the pyramid schemes? A couple of reasons really. At any given moment in the US there are around 1200 direct selling companies. Most of them fail within their first 3 years. Trust me I know. I will share that story with you in a later chapter. When a company goes out of business, people lose their jobs and sales people lose their incomes. The profession was volatile.

There were predatory owners. They started companies knowing full well that it would only last a few years, so they worked hard to make as much money as they could as fast as they could, and then they would bail. A lot of people got hurt in these scenarios. The profession started to get a bad name. This also created predatory sales people. They knew they would only be able to cash in for a few years, so they recruited people like crazy. They over promised and under delivered. They knew full well that it was a short lived 'run' and they didn't care. Some distributors made fortunes jumping from company to company making as much as they could, and leaving a trail of bodies in their wake. *This was a big contributor to the bad reputation the profession had for so long.*

However, like any naughty teenager, at some point you HAVE to grow up. **And this awesome profession HAS!** There are regulatory agencies that closely watch the profession. There is legislation that protects the consumer, the sales people and companies alike. The profession has truly COME of AGE. Pyramids are illegal. If a company has a product they are legitimately selling, and if they do not pay for recruitment, then most likely they are legal. That issue should be dead once and for all. Unfortunately, I do still see a company pop up from time to time with an owner who still uses the old school way. They massively promote the money. They make product claims. They tell you they can ship to every country in the world, etc, etc. Because of all the hype, they grow quickly, but trust me when I say this; these companies

NEVER survive! They are always gone within their first 1-3 years taking your credibility with it.

Let's tackle the MLM issue. MLM does not refer to a type of company. It ONLY refers to the method of compensation that a company offers. There are many different models that have been used over the years. A direct selling company pays the distributor for their sales of products alone. If the sales person has the ability to earn commission from people they recruit, regardless of the amount of levels, then it would be considered multi-level compensation. What is important for you to know is that you WANT your company to pay you on multiple levels of product sales. It is a GOOD thing to be involved in an MLM company. Getting paid on multiple levels of salespeople and customers is the magic fairy dust. It is the key to true leverage. Is that clear? Let's go over it again for the people in the back who can't hear as well. Pyramids are illegal. If people ask you "Is it one of those pyramid things?" You can confidently and emphatically tell them NO those are illegal. MLM is only referencing the way you may or may not get paid. So if people ask you "Is this MLM?" You can explain to them that YES, we get paid on multiple levels of sales. Or YES, we don't have a cap on the levels we get paid on, or YES, actually we get paid on an infinite number of levels of customers and sales, and it's awesome!

If I get asked that dreaded "Is this one of those pyramids" question, (I say dreaded because I know how it can trip you up when someone asks) I just say, "Are you asking me if I'm doing something illegal? Pyramids are illegal." This usually trips them up and they don't really have anything else to say, and when they do say more, they dig themselves into an even deeper hole because they usually have NO idea what they are talking about. When they get done rambling, you can then calmly continue your story of how your products and opportunity have been life changing.

You need to **know and understand these terms, and what they mean.** It will help you to not only build your confidence when you are talking to people, and it will build your OWN belief. The higher your own belief is, the more believable you are to others.

> *" The Network Marketing profession is an incredible way for the average person to take control of their own financial future "*

The Network Marketing profession is an incredible way for the average person to take control of their own financial future. It has been called the poor man's franchise because it is virtually an at home franchise model without the large startup costs, employees or expensive monthly overhead. It does not require any specific education, background or experience. You can come as you are right NOW and begin to earn while you are learning. You can authentically be who you are. It is the great equalizer. ***No matter who you are or who you were, when you start a Network Marketing business, everyone starts at the same place.*** Everyone has the same opportunity, products and compensation plan. You will earn in direct relation to the level of action and activity you engage in. If you work harder than the person who signed you up, you can earn more. How exciting is that?! You don't have to create your own marketing materials, websites or accounting systems. This is all done for you by the company. You don't have to keep inventory or stock up on products. The company also does that and they even deliver directly to your new customers for you. Most companies offer a lot of training and make most of it available for free. They know it is worth the investment to provide information and training to their sales force for free, as this allows a better chance to spread the good news about their company, products and business opportunity. This is also our philosophy as I've been mentioning.

This profession revolves around personal development. Since your ability to recruit and develop leaders on your team is directly related to your level of influence, personal development is key. I will spend an entire chapter on growing your level of influence later in the book.

Personal development and great mentorship is part of the foundation of this profession. When you fully engage, your life will change in many ways. I always tell people that Network Marketing will allow you to become the best version of yourself if you allow it to. Even if you didn't reach your financial goals, you would still receive massive rewards just by being part of the community.

I want to spend a little time explaining leverage to you. This is a very important thing for you to know and to understand. Actually, my hope is that you fall madly in love with this concept. It is this very thing that keeps the hope alive for people when they have failed or been unsuccessful in attempting to become a professional Network Marketer. Leverage! Such a beautiful word. It is a difficult thing to create in the traditional business world. There is a cost for wealth using traditional methods. If you want to make more money, you have to work more, dedicate more time and spend more precious hours of your life pursuing it. Or you can hire more people which becomes a whole new set of expensive, aggrivating problems.

It's the dream right, to be able to make more money and work less hours? Who wouldn't say yes to that?! But there are few opportunities for people to actually create it. ***Enter Network Marketing. It gleams with opportunity to create true leverage.***

Here is what it looks like:

1. Become an excited and loyal product user.

2. Share your excitement with others.

3. Teach those people to be a loyal product users, and share their excitement with others.

Sounds easy right?

Add in the chance to earn a small portion of the sales of each and every person buying and sharing those products, and you have created something magical. The idea of being able to earn income from the efforts of others who are buying, consuming and loving your products can get very exciting! You can earn over and over and over again on the continued sales of your customers and their customers. Over time you can actually build yourself an income producing asset. It creates an exciting incentive to get great at teaching others your simple business model. When you accumulate a little bit of effort from a large number of people, you create leverage. J. Paul Getty says, "I'd rather earn 1% from the efforts of 100 men than earn 100% of my own efforts." The idea of being able to leverage the efforts of a team of people who are promoting and selling your products is amazing and very exciting! This works because everyone has the same amount to gain. Someone you recruit can earn as much as you can or more if they put in more effort. This makes Network Marketing so fair and appealing. You can actually be paid for your efforts, and for your efforts of teaching and training others to do the same.

Imagine if you spent 10 hours a week building your Network Marketing business. You would be able to earn from 10 hours of effort. Now imagine that you recruited 3 people who also spent 10 hours a week on their business. Now you would be able to earn on 40 hours a week of effort while you were still only putting in just 10 of those hours. What if those 3 people each went and found 3 people themselves? That's an additional 30 hours a week of work within your business, totaling 70 hours of efforts that week in building your empire.

> *" True leverage is created when everyone involved has the same amount to gain "*

Now imagine hundreds of excited people building their own dreams, and YOU are able to earn off the efforts of the entire team. True leverage is created when everyone involved has the same amount to gain. Every person on your team has the same amount to gain with their efforts. This is what creates Network Marketing magic.

There is no "The person at the top makes all the money". In a good company, a legal company, one with a legal and ethical compensation plan, everyone has the same incentive and the same amount to gain.

It was this concept that lit me on fire for this profession. As a single Mom working 50 to 60 hours a week standing behind the chair in a salon, I heard every possible opportunity out there. I had a variety of clients who had a lot of diversity in their lives. I heard about Network Marketing and Direct Sales for a number of years. Many of them invited me to join them in their ventures. They would excitedly share their 'pitch' with me as I made their hair beautiful again. I listened with open ears. I always knew I wouldn't spend my life behind that chair. I saw career stylists who had been doing it for 20+ years and I knew that was NOT where I wanted to end up. I knew there was more available for me; I just didn't know what it was yet. So, my ears were always open to listening to what other people were up to. Of the many clients who talked to me about starting my own home business, there was one common denominator. None of them were making any significant income. Oh sure, they would tout of the friend who had a cousin who's neighbor was making $10,000 to $20,000 a month, but THEY were not making that kind of money. So to me it was all fluff. If the people I knew weren't doing it, and I had never met anyone doing it, it just wasn't real to me. It was just a fairytale. I didn't have a bad feeling about the profession, I just didn't think it was the answer I was looking for.

I was a teen Mom. I had my daughter at 16, and my son at 19. I was divorced with two small children before I turned 22. I worked in the restaurant business for a few years, and I went to one semester of college with the intent of becoming a teacher. I realized that it would take me way too many years to get that done, and I wasn't thrilled with the pay available to me either. So that was out. I decided I would enter the beauty business. I loved it! I was a total beauty product junkie and I seemed to have some natural talent.

It took me two years to get through cosmetology school. I went to school 40 hours a week, and I worked 30 to 40 hours a week at night in a restaurant/bar. As a single Mom doing all I could to make ends meet, I missed so much of my children's lives. My life consisted of doing whatever I could to make enough money to provide for my kids, and spending any extra time that I was NOT working with them. I never wanted my kids to suffer because they had such a young Mom, so I worked HARD! *I thought about our future and how I could create the kind of future where we could get rid of the money question forever.* The money question? You know the one... HOW MUCH DOES IT COST? I hated that question, and I didn't want that to be the first thing I had to ask when my kids needed or wanted something. I wanted them to have a great life and I wanted to live that life WITH them.

Standing behind the chair, I had come a long way from

working very late nights as a cocktail waitress. I was able to control my destiny to a degree. I could work long hours. I could work 7 days a week. I could charge my clients what I wanted. I built a very successful career that was earning me six figures per year, but the price for that was high. I worked a ton. I only made money while I was there, and I had topped out. I couldn't grow my income

> *" I only made money while I was there, and I had topped out. I couldn't grow my income any higher "*

any higher. I knew that in the long run this career would take its toll on my body. I was around lots of chemicals and toxins all day every day, and I was standing on my feet for 10 to 12 hours per day. It was a gigantic blessing for us, but it was NOT my long term goal.

I met my husband on a blind date. I had all but given up on dating, and was basically pushed into this blind date. It was late July of 2000. It was a Friday night, and I worked on Saturday. I was going out of obligation and I had no desire to meet the man of my dreams at that time. Fast forward ... The connection was instant. We laughed and joked like old friends. He was confident and successful and little bit cocky. Not the rude kind, but the kind that could take life with a grain of salt knowing he was in complete control of his destiny. He had a LOT of time on his hands. He would call me in the middle of the day at the salon I worked at to see what I was up too. "Umm ... well, I am at work so I am working", is what I would tell him. **His lifestyle was SO different than mine.** He had tons of time! He had a big cell phone and did meetings a few times a week in the evening, and he had a weekly conference call. He was a professional Network Marketer! At the time that we started dating he was the #2 income earner in a company that sold tax services and audit protection. I didn't know this at the time, but he was earning over $80,000 PER MONTH! No wonder he was so cocky! I went to a few of his meetings and listened in on his calls. I was intrigued by it all, but I didn't jump in. I had worked so hard to build my own business and I wasn't ready to split my focus.

A few years later life was much the same except we were now married and had a little one of our own. I had 3 kids now. My oldest was a freshman in high school, my son was in middle school and our little girl went to daycare a few days a week. Bobby had stepped out of Network Marketing and started a traditional business; a mortgage company. The days were passing by so fast. As a family on any given day we were off in five different directions. My oldest daughter Bree played basketball and I was only able to go to one game. ONE GAME! I was missing their lives... STILL! I had already missed so much and

I was determined not to miss anymore. A white hot fire began to burn deep inside of me. It gave me a powerful sense of urgency that if I didn't make a change, and fast, my children were going to grow up and move out. They would have never known me, and I wouldn't know them. I felt desperate and rushed! I felt like time was going to run out. ***I needed to do something NOW!***

A client and friend of mine had been prospecting me for her Network Marketing business every 4 to 6 weeks when she came in to get her hair done. She continued to do this for 18 months. She would sit in my chair and tell me how awesome I would be and how great she was doing! She had a bright and cheery personality and was very cute and personable. It was the last day of May of 2004 when she sat in my chair and proceeded to talk through her normal speech yet again. But on this day, I was hurried. I was feeling the pressure of needing a change in my life. On that day I wasn't wanting to hear the speech, I wanted to hear solutions. So I said to her, "If you want me in your business so bad, then I need to know, how much are you making?" I only asked this of her because we were friends for a number of years at that point, and for me, starting another business was only about one thing; THE MONEY! I wasn't looking for an extra few hundred dollars a month. That would not have changed my current situation. I was looking to significantly impact my finances. I was looking to even replace my income. That was the ONLY way I could change my story. She said, "Well I made $13,000 this month." I was shocked! In 18 months, she created a six-figure income with zero experience! Needless to say, the timing was right for me.

Something in me shifted in that moment. I knew that if SHE could do that, so could I. And I believed I could do it in half the time. I had my mentor sleeping next to me every night. I knew this was going to free me. With Bobby's help and mentorship, I cannonballed into the profession. I was ignorance on fire! We built a six-figure income with that company in 9 months. I was in love with the profession. I have now built three separate businesses to multiple six figure incomes totaling millions of dollars. I also worked on the corporate side for a short period of time. In 2010 we started our own company with the help of investors. That lasted two and a half years and ended ugly. In 2012 we came back to our roots and built a million-dollar business again. We've seen the good, the bad and the ugly, but in the end, the bad and ugly are still better than working 40 to 60 hours a week away from my family, driving in traffic, working with people we don't like in a profession we aren't passionate about. Network Marketing offers a promise of freedom and self-reliance when it is done right. ***My passion is burning brighter now than it was when I began my career. I stand proud for this profession and what it can do when it is done right.***

Over the years I have truly seen it all in this profession. I have never had an advantage. I have built one person at a time against all odds. The remainder of this book will be me sharing with you the steps, tools and skills it takes to build your empire. I am glad for all the obstacles I have faced. They have served as a massive training ground. I want more to people to be equipped to change their own lives. I do not believe that our purpose on this planet is to get jobs, go to work to pay the bills for 40+ years of our lives, and then retire not knowing our children or our spouses. And most people have to retire on half or less of the income they earned while they were working. That system feels broken to me! I believe there is so much more. I also believe that this profession will continue to be the answer for millions of people around the globe.

" *My passion is burning brighter now than it was when I began my career. I stand proud for this profession and what it can do when it's done right* "

Think Like An Entrepreneur

Chapter 2

"Entrepreneurs are the only ones who'll work 80 hours a week, to avoid working 40." – Lori Grenier

Y ou signed up in a Network Marketing company ... now you're an entrepreneur! Well, maybe not. According to the dictionary, an entrepreneur is someone who is willing to put up a financial risk and operate a business. When you sign up with a Direct Selling/Network Marketing company, you are purchasing products that you will use. You will (hopefully) really enjoy the products you purchase, and receive a great benefit from them. In addition to that, if you don't love them, almost all legitimate companies have a return policy or a buy back policy, or both. So what real risk are you taking? I'll answer that for you. NONE. You are taking NO risk. If you don't like what you've purchased, you can return it for a partial or full refund. There is virtually ZERO financial risk to you. Let's be honest, MOST people are not entrepreneurs, nor do they know what it means to be one, or how to pursue business as an entrepreneur. So how can we expect people to know what it means to build a business in this profession. The bottom line is we can't. ***We need to do a much better job teaching people what it means, what it takes, and most of all how to shift their thinking from employee to entrepreneur.***

We set ourselves and our team up for failure when do not manage their expectations. If you wanted to be a Doctor, you would know there is a specific path you'd have to take. There is a large investment of time and money into your education and training before you can ever diagnose a patient, or even make a dollar as a Doctor. If you want a be a Lawyer, you need to go to college, law school, and pass the bar before you can defend a case as a Lawyer. When I went to cosmetology school, it took an investment of 1600 hours of education before I could take the state licensing exam. Then I had to be an assistant before I could ever take on my own clients. Just about any and every type of job imaginable requires a significant amount of training before you can 'begin' the job. And any profession that has the potential to pay you six figures a year or more, requires a lot of time and training. This is not only accepted, it is celebrated. Just go tell someone that you've decided to go back to college. Tell them you're going to invest six figures into your education for the next 6 or more years so that you can earn more at your job or start a new career, and people will throw you a party. They will celebrate you and your decision. No one in their right mind would ask you two or three months into your journey, how much money you were making, or how much success you've had. They understand that you are investing in a better future. They even edify you for going into debt and spending such a large amount of your time in order to have a better future.

But join a Network Marketing company and see how quickly the standards change. If someone isn't making $10k a month within their first six months, people scoff and sneer. They tell people ahh well nothing happened, so it must be a scam. They say these 'things' don't work so they quit. Mind you, those same people never took the time to be trained, learn and actually treat it like a real profession, or a viable career. They joined, used a few products, and maybe looked at a website or got on a team call. They talked to a few people with little or no training, heard two or three no's and decided it doesn't work. Why do we have such a different standard? Why have we put Network Marketing in its own category of standards of time and financial investment? This is a career where you can create an income larger than a Doctor, a Lawyer or even the President of the United States. BUT it will require some time, education and some skill building. It is up to *US* to help change the way we and others look at this profession.

I have listened to many million-dollar earners say that

when they started, they had a several year plan to make it work. They did NOT tell themselves they would give it 3 to 6 months, and if it didn't work in that short time frame they would quit. They decided from the beginning they would give it 3 years, 5 years or 10 years to create the income and lifestyle they desired. Can you make money fast in this profession? Oh yes you sure can, but this is really about the long game. You must come into this profession with a career mindset. If you have a hobby mindset, you'll be paid a hobby income. If you have the long game in mind and a career mindset, the sky's the limit!

> *" Entrepreneurs think about time and money much differently "*

You may be an ***accidental-preneur***. You signed up, consumed some great products, got results and people wouldn't stop asking you about them, so you decided to give the business a shot.

Or maybe you're a ***wanna-preneur***. You love the idea of being an independent business owner, but you have never owned a business. You don't know what it takes because you've always had a boss guiding you.

If either of those describes you, or some variation of each, you'll need to begin to change your thinking. You'll need to start thinking like an entrepreneur. Entrepreneurs think about time and money much differently. It isn't linear. It is all about the investment and the return on that investment. ***An entrepreneur realizes that you'll invest more time, energy and money on the front end, but over time that will flip.*** Let's talk specifically about being a Network Marketing entrepreneur. In the beginning you will be investing time, and not being paid in relation to the time you're putting in. For those who think like employees, this is a hard stage to get past. They calculate the amount of time spent working their business and the amount they earn, and they see that their current job or profession is probably paying them more. They decide it isn't worth it and they quit. This is the WRONG way to look at it. That way of thinking is why the great majority of people never earn the bigger incomes available to them. In the Network Marketing profession, if you can stick it out longer and just keep going, those numbers will change dramatically.

For example, if you are working your Network Marketing business 15 hours a week consistently for the first 6 months, and you average $1000 - $2000 a month over that period of time, you would be earning between $16 - $33 dollars per hour. Not bad. Now imagine in two years you're still working 15 hours per week, but now you're earning $7000 - $10,000 a month. You'd be earning $117 - $166 per hour. I'd say that is quite a raise. The amount of hours you've invested hasn't changed, but the team has grown and you are able to earn on the accumulated efforts of them. ***An entrepreneur understands that there is always an upfront investment of time, money and sweat equity FIRST before the rewards start pouring in.*** Think about this; when an airplane takes off, it uses the majority of its fuel on the takeoff. It requires the most energy to get that enormous metal tube up off the ground and into the sky. This is the same concept for business ownership and Network Marketing.

I have been using work hours in these examples, but I want to make a slight shift here. While there is an investment of time required, you can compress the time required and create acceleration in the growth of your business. In Network Marketing it's not HOW LONG you've been in the business, it's HOW MANY. I'll repeat that, it's not how long, it's how many. If you want your business to grow with speed, increase the amount of people you talk to and enroll. That is a very important tip. There are scores of people who have been in Network Marketing for 2 to 6 years and still have not earned more than a few thousand dollars a month. Ask them how many people they are talking to every day or week, as well as how many they have enrolled in the last 30 to 60 days. I would be willing to bet it is not very many, if any at all. On the flip side of that, ask a six-figure earner how many people they enrolled in the first 12 to 18 months of their business and most will tell you it is 100+. If this is a numbers game, and the numbers have always seemed to hold up, then you can easily figure out how to speed up the process for yourself. Truth be told, the ONLY way to speed up the growth of your business is to talk to more people, faster.

TIP: To speed up the process of building your business, talk to MORE people.

Another important part of your investment into your Network Marketing career is your company's events. Over the years I have seen it again and again. People desperately want to earn a full time income for their families, and yet they are not willing to invest in the training required to take themselves or their business to the next level. Your company events are not a nice little party you get invited to that you can either attend or miss on a whim. Your company events are a non-negotiable if you are trying to make this your career with a significant income. The cost to attend a Network Marketing corporate event is pennies on the dollar compared to any other personal or skill development event outside of this profession. Personal growth and skill development events can cost thousands or even tens of thousands of dollars. I know this because I have attended many of them. There is no comparison with the price of events your company puts on which may cost you just few hundred dollars. Trust me when I tell you that your company puts on those events FOR YOUR benefit. Those events are not profitable for the company. They are solely for the growth and benefit of the distributors (You). You should view these as the cost of doing business, and you should immediately begin to teach your business partners the same thing. Your income growth will be in direct relation to the amount of your team that attends a company event. This is a fact. You should teach yourself and your team that event attendance is not a sacrifice, but an investment, and a very worthy one at that. The more people you get to your company's large corporate events, the larger your income will grow.

A Network Marketing entrepreneur needs to have a patient sense of urgency. Oxymoron? No, and here is why. You NEED to build your business with a sense of urgency that will create energy, and that creates synergy which is a lot of activity in a lot of places within your team. The patience part comes in knowing that building a residual empire takes time. Most companies have a compensation structure that is built to keep you working and getting paid while the network of customers and consumers is growing. That network is what will provide the leverage and freedom you desire. Until that happens, you will be building in the trenches, continuing to enroll and develop leaders. I call it patient urgency.

We call this profession Net**WORK** Marketing for a reason. It takes work, and a lot of it! 'In the trenches' is something Bobby has been saying for a long time. Think of trench work on really hard ground. Pick and shovel, not really getting anywhere until you soak it with water to make it softer. At the beginning of your journey in this profession it can feel just like this. It can feel impossible sometimes right? Unfamiliar territory, uncertainty, even disappointment. Just know that over time (Soaking the ground) it does get easier. You become more familiar, certain and confident just like you have in the past when you've started a new job. Give it time!

You must train your brain to think outside the box of what is 'normal.' You need to open up some space inside of your mind to allow for you to do things differently than you have done in the past. You need to understand that in order to create a full-time income, you must be open to doing different things for your business than you have done as an employee. Change is hard for most people; really hard, and sometimes virtually impossible actually. They begin to change, and that feels weird, so they feel like they need to return to what feels comfortable. ***As a new Network Marketing entrepreneur, you must accept and even enjoy the fact that you are going to be OUT OF YOUR COMFORT zone for a period of time.*** The path that most of us have been taught to follow is NOT the only path. Shark Tank star Kevin O'Leary says, "People don't start a business out of greed or for the money, they do it for the free-dom." We are willing to work harder, knowing that the payoff we earn is much more than financial. In Network Marketing this is why finding a mentor is so crucial. Every single success story has this in common. They all had someone, or multiple someone's who coached and guided them. They found someone who had something they wanted. Knowledge, success, a system, a path that worked, and they learned everything they could from that person. Network Marketing is the only profession I have found that has that system built in. You don't have to pay big bucks to be mentored. You can search your upline (If you're already in a company) for someone successful who has a vested interest in your success. If you are NOT signed up in a company yet, be selective with whom you partner with. ***IT MATTERS***! Make sure that you will be able to have access to someone who will willingly and passionately mentor you. As a leader myself, I love nothing more than to find people on my team who are hungry and coachable.

That leads me into a very important part of being a Network Marketing entrepreneur. This profession attracts people of every walk of life, every level of success, and every possible profession. Sometimes when someone comes from a very successful background into this profession, we think this will be an easy shift for them. If they were successful at their current career, they will easily be successful with this one. I have seen this happen. Someone with success and influence can jump into Network Marketing and grow a team with a lot of speed. And I have also seen them fall flat on their face as well. One very important character trait of a successful entrepreneur is being coachable. If someone's past success has led to arrogance or ego, they will not be open to learning how THIS profession works, and no level of previous success will carry over into this new venture. It is never easy to start at the bottom, especially if you are at the top of your game and making a lot of money in your current career, or have received any level of recognition. Trust me on this one.

> *" One very important character trait of a successful entrepreneur is being coachable "*

When Bobby and I started our own Network Marketing company, I felt I had arrived. All that we had been through together as a couple and on our own, had led us to this massive opportunity. We were going to be able to create something that would last a lifetime and help thousands of families along the way. God had given us a very clear vision of our mission and we were passionate about seeing it through. Bobby was Co-Founder and CEO and I was Co-Founder and President. Me, a teen Mom who came from nothing, had overcome MANY obstacles and a lot of adversity, was the Co-Founder and President of my very own company in a profession I loved! It was surreal. For 2.5 years we burned the candle at both ends. We ran the office and corporation side during the day, and we built the distributors side at night and on weekends just like a traditional Networker. It was a very humble start. I told people it was a labor of love because it was NOT freedom. It was 18 hour days, never ending work and very little budget. But we had our sights on the vision and we did it without complaint. Our little company slowly grew. We had created an incredible culture and a loyal team that felt more like a family to us than a business. This made it very difficult to acknowledge when we both began to feel something wasn't right. We did not want to admit that things were changing. Our relationship with our investors felt strained. I won't bore you with details but the bottom line is this, we had partnered with a group of people who never intended for us to see our vision to fruition. They sought out people like Bobby and I; ambitious, energetic, successful team leaders who could build the distributor base. Then at some point, they would drop the leaders and keep the distributors. They would absorb the smaller companies into the older larger company they owned to try to keep a dying company alive with these 'injections' of new customers. Of course we did NOT know any of this at the time. It was a brutal lesson to learn!

Then D day came. We sat down on a Friday morning in Salt Lake City Utah for our quarterly board meeting. Bobby and I were excited to share new Marketing materials and training we had created to help our growing company. We had spent several months creating a system for our distributors to follow, and we would present it to the board that day. But.... We never had the chance to do that. Within the first 5 minutes of the board meeting, we were told they were changing directions and we were no longer included in the plans. Talk about a punch to the gut. I went numb. In one fell swoop everything we had poured into our company was gone. They owned more of the business than we did, so they had the ability to vote us out. I will never forget that day. It shaped many things about who I am today. For 2.5 years both Bobby and I had contacted every single person we had ever known and invited them on the journey with us. We told them that with us as owners, we could ensure that we would do the right thing for them and always put their interests first. We promised integrity and heart above greed and backstabbing. We even had a Bible verse on the back of every product and box. Isaiah 43: 18-19 which reads:

> "Forget the former things; do not dwell on the past. See, I am doing a new thing! Now it springs up; do you not perceive it? I am making a way in the wilderness and streams in the wasteland."

And in an instant, it was all gone. Not only was our dream dead, so was the dream of thousands of others who followed and believed us. I was devastated and humiliated at the same time. The so called new direction the board wanted to go in fell apart in the next 90 days, and the company along with our dream went away.

Where do you go from there? What is the next step for a former CEO & President of a company? We had built 2 organizations together to a six figure a year income, and we had owned our own Network Marketing company. What could be next? Starting back at the bottom? When we decided what our next steps were, we considered a lot of options. Staying on the corporate side of the profession, I could go back to doing hair, or we could go back to being distributors and build another team. We chose the latter. We decided to give it one more try and build a team again. I still had belief in the profession. *I hung on to the sliver of hope that I had left and we got started...again...at the bottom, just like everyone else.* We didn't start with a new company trying to be experts or know-it-alls. We didn't rely on our past success as the thing we talked about. We yielded to the successful upline and we became the best students. We were completely coachable to the ways of the company we chose, to the ways of the team we were on, and we followed diligently. Did we know how to build teams? Of course we did. We had done it more than once with incredible success. Both Bobby and I were smart enough, and humble enough to know that in order to be successful with this new company we chose, we had to follow the leader. Being able to allow someone with more success, with a path available for you to follow is not about being a follower, it is about being a leader. A leader with enough sense to know, that you don't know everything.

So, we dug in, listened and learned, and we followed so that we could lead. Really think about that for a second before you read on.

TIP: If you want to lead and be an exceptional leader, you must first be an exceptional follower.

Entrepreneurs do not see failure like most people do. They see what the world would call 'failure' as one way that didn't work. Those times do not derail an entrepreneur, they DRIVE them to try again and learn from what didn't work. If your desire or your WHY is big enough, those failures don't even phase you. You get back up and try again, and this time with more knowledge and skill. I like to call what happened to us, THE BEST WORST THING that ever happened. Some of my closest friends came from that company, and some of my biggest learning opportunities. I am so glad it happened because it led us to the place we are today. We are living examples of all that is possible in Network Marketing. It isn't an overnight success. It has been a battle of circumstances and obstacles that we made it through. I wouldn't have it any other way!

" *If your desire or your WHY is big enough, failures don't even phase you. You get back up and try again - this time with more knowledge and skill* "

Getting Started

Chapter 3

"By failing to prepare, you are preparing to fail."
– Benjamin Franklin

*T*here are a handful of things you can do RIGHT now to set yourself up for success. They are seemingly so simple, but it is because of that simplicity that many times we fail to teach this to our newest team members. I have been guilty of this MANY times over the years. I assume that people know how and what to do to prepare, and get things a little bit organized. The fact is that VERY often, not only do they not do it, they don't even know what to do. I am going to give you some very basic tips at getting organized. Just enough to begin growing your business. Then I am going to give you some steps to take to get the ball rolling:

1. Your work space.

It is very important that you have a space to work in.

In Network Marketing you'll need to have a calendar, a place to make calls, a place to keep track of your prospects and team members etc, so a designated space is important. Let's not get too crazy. If you don't have a home office, no worries. I have used a space in my kitchen, a desk in my bedroom and many other various spaces in my home, as well as dedicating a room to be an office over the years. Most importantly, you need an area to keep track of things. Being organized is very subjective. To some, I am really organized, and to others I am a hot mess. The only thing that matters is that you are organized FOR YOU. We all lead very busy lives and without at least a little bit of structure, things can easily fall through the cracks. So set aside a place where you can get things done, have a few files or notebooks, and your laptop or desktop computer.

2. Designated work hours.

Now I will talk a lot about being able to grow your business in the cracks of your day, and this is still 100% true. But I also like to teach people to set aside time each week to dedicate to their business. Decide how many hours you have to use specifically for growing your business, then block that time out on your calendar. I still use a paper calendar. I have tried to use an automated one, but I didn't like them. I live and die by what I write in my calendar. I will ask my brand new people how much time they will be able to spend on building their business every week. This helps me to help them with their goals.

Next you need to write down or set up reminders for any and all teams calls, corporate calls, team and company events for the next 12 months. Putting them on your calendar will help you to stay on task, and remind you to build in time for these important events. I like using block scheduling. I think for most people this helps clear the clutter of the mind and will allow you to focus on specific things at specific times. This is very much how men work. They don't overdo things with multi-tasking. They focus on one task, give it 100% and when they are done, they move on to the next task. For people with busy lives, block scheduling can clear a path for them to be 100% present in what they are doing.

3. Tech.

Most companies have websites and apps. Make sure to know what these are by either downloading or book-marking them. These are your business tools, and they will make your job of learning as well as teaching and prospecting others much easier. Allow the tools to do the work for you. This allows you to leverage yourself and others.

4. Notebooks & whiteboards.

Because you will be prospecting a lot of new people, you need a simple and consistent way to keep track of all of them. I use 5x7 note cards and a recipe box. (You can see details on my YouTube channel) Some people use notebooks and some use contact management systems. There are many ways to keep track of the people you are talking to. It doesn't matter what system you choose, just choose one and use it like your life depends on it. Your business depends on you connecting with people, developing a relationship and then following up with them again and again. You will be giving yourself an incredible advantage when you have kept notes on each person, and are able to recall details they shared with you, and even that you remembered them in the first place. In addition to my recipe box filing system, I always have a white board in my office to keep people's names in front of me. My hot prospects and my brand new people go on that board so I can serve them as needed, and no one gets forgotten due to lack of organization. This is a small investment of time and money for something that will yield you a large return.

5. Lifelines.

In Network Marketing you will be learning as you are growing. Your life will depend on your ability to connect with your mentor/active upline for help and questions on the fly. I always recommend that you have at least three lifeline phone numbers available to you. These people will be your lifeline for training, getting your questions answered and support. Save these numbers in your phone and make them a favorite so you will have easy access to them. You may also want to save your company's customer service number, and your team conference call numbers as well. This small step will help tremendously if you're in a pinch.

These are just a few simple things you need to do right away to set yourself up for success. It will make your life much easier in the long run to do these things now, and have a few systems in place for keeping yourself organized.

Next, I am going to give you some basic steps for getting started with your business. These will be generic in nature because I want you to know that I believe you will find more speed and efficiency by plugging in to your team or company system. That being said, the fundamentals don't really vary or change much.

1. Your product testimonial.

This may seem like a stupid thing to write, but because I believe that today's consumer is more moved by your story than by facts, I think this is key to having a successful start to your business. So whatever product your company offers, be your own best customer. Use it correctly, and use it daily with the intention of getting fabulous results. Make sure that you authentically love it as well as know what it has done for you and your life. When you do this, it will not only be natural to talk about it, it will be hard not to. This will create organic interest and excitement around what you're doing.

2. *Your WHY.*

This is VERY important. Why are you doing this? Why did you start using the products? Why do you want to grow this into a business? What would more income do for you and your family? What would you do if you woke up tomorrow with no bills, had plenty of money, and didn't have to go to a job? What are you passionate about? Not only do YOU need to be able to answer those questions, but you need to be able to share them. Without a strong reason WHY, it is easy to put your business on the back burner, and then put it in a box on a shelf and forget about it. But a strong emotional reason WHY will keep you going on the hard days. Write down your why for you to see every day, then share it with your active upline who is coaching and mentoring you.

3. *Circle of trust.*

No matter who you are, we all have a circle of trust. These are the people we go to for advice, mentoring, friendship and fun. These are the people we do life and work with. These people are our family and friends. You are going to begin a list of names and these are the people who you are going to write down first. These people are your supporters and encouragers. Even if they don't jump on board with your vision of the future, they will be cheering you on from the sidelines.

4. The list.

If you don't have a list, you don't have a business. This is about as true as it gets. Your list is never ending and you will never stop adding names to the list, and the only reason you take people off that list is when they become your customer or partner in business. I like to use a physical list with handwritten names. Then I transfer those names to my filing system once I have contacted them, so I can keep track of our conversations. You can type the names out in an excel or word file. I don't care how you create this list, but you need a list. I suggest starting with 100 names. I know that made you panic a little, but look at the number of contacts in your smartphone contacts right now. I would be willing to bet you have a minimum of 300. A list of 100 names should be very easy in today's age of technology. This list will change your life as well as the lives of the people on your list, so do not leave anyone off the list. Rule #1 – It is not for you to decide who says yes and who says no. You need to give everyone the same opportunity and let THEM decide. Your job is to put them on the list, that it all.

5. Goals and commitments.

Because you are brand new, you won't know exactly how to set goals for your business. Each company will have specific levels to reach for you to receive bonuses, trips, incentives and rank advancements. Your mentor will help you to map this out and set specific target dates on them. What you WILL know is what you want to accomplish in the next 12 months, meaning, you can easily decide your financial goal. How much would you like to be earning in 12 months? Your mentor will take that goal and work backwards to help you clearly see the path to reach it. Having a clear set of goals is important. It has been proven time and time again that a written down goal has about a 78% chance of being accomplished, and if you tell someone else about that goal, the percentage goes even higher. In addition to setting goals with dates, you will want to tell your enroller what you are committed to. Example: I am committed to reaching out to 15 new people per week. I am committed to spending 15 hours per week working on my business. I am committed to hosting one presentation per week. These are a few examples of what you can and should be committing to with your enroller. Lastly, I would suggest that you commit to touching base with him/her every day. This person is your PARTNER, and they are in the trenches WITH you. They have a vested interest in your success. It is YOUR job to stay connected to them and learn from them. A good upline will pour everything they have learned into you and guide you to each next step. But remember, they are NOT your boss or manager. It is your job to grow your business, but the amazing and encouraging news is, you are NOT ALONE doing it.

6. Your first win.

This step is crucial. You will learn so much by taking

this step as fast as you can. Everyone has a few people in their circle of trust who will ALWAYS support you and who will ALWAYS join you. It could be a new fitness class, a great book, a movie you recommended or a great new show on Netflix. These people are ALL IN with you. You are going to utilize your mentor/upline/enroller to help you get your first win. After you've made your Circle of Trust list, you are going to contact them WITH YOUR ENROLLER. Do not attempt to do this on your own yet. Allow your mentor to do their job and do all of the talking for you. The conversation would look something like this whether it is via text/call/message:

> "Hi Billy, You already know I have been miserable with my job. I have been searching for a way to transition into something new for a while. Well recently I was introduced to _____ product and I've had AMAZING results! (Now share your results with the product/service) In addition to that, I got in contact with _____ (Enroller/mentors name) and they have been helping me. [Here is where you will edify your enrollers success] I have him/her on the phone with us now. I have decided to turn my results into revenue. Of course, you are at the TOP of my list of people I'd love to work with, and I know you have also been wanting a change and have been looking for ways to earn more money."

Once you do this introduction you allow your successful experienced upline to handle the remainder of the call. Mute your phone, listen, takes notes and learn. (These are excellent training calls for you to learn how to do it, so you can in turn do it for your team.) They should know exactly how to handle this call. I do these over a 3-way phone call, or over any form of video call like Zoom or Facetime. I love to do video calls because it allows for a more personal and real connection. It is as close as face to face as you can get. And because people are so busy these days, they are a great way to connect to save time.

> *" This is not a one-man show, this business is designed to be built with a team and teamwork "*

A few things happen when you use this method for reaching out. First, you are learning from every call. You will hear answers to the most commonly asked questions, how to engage and talk with people. Second, you are showing your friend and future business partner that you are not doing this business on your own because you have a support team of people who are helping you. They know you are new at it, and they know you don't know the answers, but now they see that even with your newbie status, you are still moving forward and pursuing your dreams. This is a very powerful thing you'll be teaching them. Next, it teaches you how to leverage the skills of other people on your team. This is not a one man show, this business is designed to be built with a team and teamwork. Remember, everything you do is teaching your new business partner.

Your goal should be to do 10 of these types of calls as fast as possible. This will set the stage for success and duplication in your business. In truth, we are just a bunch of copycats. Our goal is not to reinvent how to create the residual life, it is to duplicate the steps your successful upline took to build theirs. You will hear the word duplication A LOT in this profession. Eric Worre says, "It's not what works, it is what duplicates, that matters in this business." This means that you could have a specific set of talents or skills, or a special level of influence that brings you success in your business, but if the people on your team cannot effectively duplicate what YOU did to create that success themselves, then your team will NOT grow. Follow the successful steps of the leader. This makes your business easier to grow and a lot more fun. You do NOT have to be an expert to grow your business. What you need to be is an expert at knowing what tools to use and what steps to follow. Having a team system makes all the difference. You will read more about that in a later chapter.

The faster I can get someone through the steps already listed in this chapter, the more excitement and momentum they will build. If it takes someone 60 days to get through them, the likelihood of them being a serious business building partner goes down.

" You do NOT have to be an expert to grow your business. What you need to be is an expert at knowing what tools to use & what steps to follow "

Raising Your Influence

Chapter 4

"Example is not the main thing in influencing others, it's the only thing." – Albert Schweitzer

*I*nfluence – the capacity to have an effect on the character, development, or behavior of someone or something."

When I am given the gift of a new business partner who has a large circle of influence, I throw a small party and do a happy dance around my house. I do this because I know how many lives will be impacted as a result. Ok no happy dance, but inside I am very excited. A person of influence is usually someone who has a reputation for being successful, and is very credible in his or her field of expertise. They have become known for their skills, personality, and their following, or just because people flat out like him/her. I talked about this in an earlier chapter calling them INFLUENCERS. We live in a time where people aspire to be an influencer on social media. There are people on YouTube right now who are influencing the buying habits of millions of people by reviewing and using products. It is not a new concept, but I think now we are so hyper aware of it because we are so involved with social media in our everyday lives, and because there are a lot of people making a lot of money as influencers.

In Network Marketing your level of influence will directly affect the level of success you have in your business. It could be that you have influence on just a few people. Those few people will listen to your words and advice, and they will follow it without hesitation. Or maybe you have a larger sphere of influence. Perhaps you can influence forty or four hundred people with just a simple post on social media. When you put your stamp on something, people take that as a reliable and credible opinion, and they feel safe and excited to follow your lead. That is influence. If you have zero influence or zero people that would follow you, then it is time to re- evaluate where you're at with some or all of the choices you have made up until now. Start reading books on personal growth and development so that you can start creating new habits that can change the direction of your life. ***When your direction changes for the better, people notice.*** That could be the beginning of you becoming an influencer to more people.

When people get started in their Network Marketing

business, their first level of success will be because of their influence alone. With a background as an expert in the field of beauty, my level of influence was high when I jumped into this profession and started promoting a line of skincare and cosmetics. People knew that I was an expert in that field, and if I said that a product was great, and that I used it exclusively and recommended it to them, they were eager to try it sight unseen. My credibility was high because people knew my background as a stylist and make-up artist. I was a discerning consumer and particular about what I used, so if I liked it, the general consensus was that it must be good.

Unique to this profession and a handful of others however, is the fact that no matter what profession you have come from, no matter where you have built your credibility, that influence can and will transfer over to help you build your business. In the example above, my transition seemed easier because it also involved the beauty industry. But Network Marketing breaks the rules. The only thing it asks of you is influence, no matter how it was grown. ***A successful and credible person can walk into this profession and leverage their influence from ANY previous profession, and immediately have some level of success.*** Partnering with influencers is an exciting way to build your business. Many times, people of influence know other people of influence. I have seen people's business's explode with activity when this happens!

Your current level of influence will determine the

amount of success you will have when you get started. The number of personal enrollments you have in the first 90 days can launch your business into action that will catapult your success. There comes a point in time in everyone's business where you need to grow your influence and develop your new skills to the next level in order to grow your business. I have signed up some very influential people over the years. They were leaders and had extensive spheres of influence. Each of them had immediate success and were able to enroll a greater than average number of people.

> *" Your current level of influence will determine the amount of success you will have when you get started "*

Their success was encouraging, and I was very excited for them! And then... it happened. The time came on their journey where in order for them to continue enrolling people into their business, they needed to grow and/or develop more skills. They had leveraged their influence as far as it could go at its current level. What had come so easily to them before, now seemed much harder. Sadly, for some this is where their Network Marketing journey ends. When faced with the fact that change in some form needs to occur, they choose the easier path. I am disappointed to say that I have lost a number of influential people to their lack of willingness to change or grow. It is right here in the growth phase where you will learn to develop the skills it takes to grow a large and lasting Network Marketing business.

For those who start their journey with little to no influence, this type of growth must happen right away, or they have very little chance for success. I almost think these people have a bit of an advantage. They didn't have the luxury of fast success, and they had to begin the process of growing their skills and influence immediately. Influencers can hide behind the mask of fast success, and because of that they don't always need to develop skills early on. When that day comes, instead of seeing the need and the ultimate benefits of growth, they decide Network Marketing is no longer working. It couldn't possibly be because they need to change anything about themselves or that they need to grow. It must be that this profession just doesn't work. (Insert heavy sigh and eye roll)

No matter which category you fall into, **there WILL come a day when your influence alone is NOT enough to keep your business growing. You will need to expand both your skills and your influence.** How exactly do you accomplish that? Next, I will show you a few ways to do just that, and along the way pick up some incredible skills. Here is the question you need to ask yourself. Who am I right now? And who do I need to become? Much of this is a matter of character. Since this profession is made up of a volunteer army, leadership is much different than in the traditional business and job world. Boss/employee tactics will not work to grow a team. Before I get into some of this, remember what I said at the beginning of the book. If you allow it to, this profession will help you to become the very best version of yourself. It will place a mirror right in front of you, exposing who you are and what needs to change and or shift in order to keep growing.

What would others say about you? Are you an optimist or a pessimist? Does your energy bring people up or down? This one is BIG for me. I love to surround myself with people who are positive. I can only spend limited amounts of time with people who always see the worst in life. Part of being a leader and raising your own levels of influence with others is how others feel as a result of being around you. You will not be able to influence others if they feel like crap after talking to you. Do you gossip about others or do you always point out people's faults? Do you complain a lot? Are you the person who sees the good in everything? Do you encourage others? Do you try to help point out the positives in any situation, or do you point out the negatives? The thing about energy, either good or bad, is that it is all contagious. ***You are always either affecting people or infecting people***. This is a great place to start when working on raising your level of influence. Awareness is key. Take note of how often you think or speak negative to yourself or others. The Bible says we have the authority to take each thought captive. This tells me that no matter how much we are told that we are born with a specific tendency, we can change the way we look at the world, and in turn become beacons of positive energy and growth. Marvin Ashton says "Leave people better than you found them." What an incredible mantra for life! No matter where you go or what you do, make sure to leave those in your path better than you found them. How do you do that? Speak life into others! Just a small word of encouragement can set off a chain reaction of goodness in people's lives. Random acts of kindness, no matter how small, can leave a massive impact on others. You need to become the person that people are excited to be around, and that just being in your presence makes them feel great. Never speak ill of others. Call out the gold in others instead of noticing the dirt. Do your best to seek out the lessons in loss and trials. Cast a vision for others for a better future. Be a great listener and be authentic.

TIP: When you become a person that makes others feel better just by being in your presence, your level of influence will expand.

Are you a person of your word? Do you make plans then cancel or just not show up? Are you late all the time?

Are you hard to get in touch with? These are important things to look at. If you are going to influence others, they need to be able to trust what you say. People NEED to be able to believe that if you say you'll do something, you will actually do it. You are either building a relationship of trust or you're building one of doubt. Leaders and influencers alike are people others can count on and trust. Trust is built one interaction at a time. If you said you'd call someone on a certain day or at a specific time, you'd better be sure to do that. If you have a meeting set up, be early and be prepared. Whether you want to admit it or not, every interaction you have with others is telling them a lot about who you are. People trust someone who walks their own talk. If you are promoting a healthy lifestyle, yet you yourself are not healthy or are not pursuing health, then people will have a hard time trusting what you say regarding health. People just cannot trust someone who is flakey and unreliable, no matter how much they like you. If you are not proving to them that you are worthy of their trust, you will have a very hard time influencing them. You are leaving them a lot of room for doubt. And just like the U.S. Justice system, we cannot have more than a reasonable doubt when it comes to trust. You may yourself be a distrusting person because of past experiences, but if your actions in life match your words, you are helping others to feel safe and confident with you.

Be someone who is so consistent it is annoying.
For the last 6 years of our lives, Bobby and I have been

dedicated to our own fitness and health in a BIG way. We workout 4 to 6 days a week and have not missed even when we have been on vacation. It has become a major part of our lives. A few months ago, I was on a call with my Mom and she asked me, "What are you doing right now? I said, "I'm at the gym." She replied, "Jeez you are so consistent it is annoying." I was very excited to hear that! Yes I am! I am consistent in most areas of my life. I show up at the gym, I continue to pursue incredible health, I read a lot, I show up on calls, I attend events, I answer my phone, I respond to texts, I answer emails and I keep doing that day after day, year after year. I am so consistent I annoy myself sometimes. Be YOUR WORD!

TIP: Be a person who exemplifies consistency in all areas of your life. This one trait alone will yield massive results and rewards.

What is your level of financial stability? Have you jumped from job to job? Have you started a handful of different careers, but never stuck with them long enough to have had any significant success? Are you always broke? Are you a good steward with what you do have, whether it is a little or a lot? All of these things are telling a story to others about your ability to influence them with financial decisions. As a Network Marketing influencer that is exactly what you're trying to do. If you are always broke and struggling, you will have a low level of influence. In order to right that financial imbalance as quickly as possible while you are building your business, you will need to make some changes such as lowering your debt to income ratio as quickly as you can. Learn to live on a budget and take excellent care of the things you have. Living below your means paints a picture of conscience respect for money, instead of barely making ends meet with your current income. If you have jumped from job to job, or opportunity to opportunity, you will have to work a little harder and longer in order for people to feel your advice in this area is credible. Don't fret over this. Just realize the reality of the decisions you have made. You have been showing people one thing and now you need to show them something different. Become the poster child for loyalty, consistency and perseverance. ***Over time, people will see something NEW in you, and your ability to influence them will prevail.***

Have you changed careers again and again, struggling to find your perfect fit? There is nothing wrong with that. Just be aware that people know that about you. In order for them to feel safe in following your lead, they need to feel confident that you will stick it out for once. People want to sign up with and work with leaders they think will withstand the test of time. Even if you have not had success or been a person who has made great money, that doesn't mean you cannot BECOME one. Your life is a living example for others to see. Start today and make the changes. Dave Ramsey has some incredible programs that will teach you about money and how to best to manage it. Stay the course. It will take time for you to change your own financial situation and become someone that others will look up to. Become a person with the lifestyle they want to emulate. I know many people who earn yearly six figure incomes, and yet they are always broke. I had a friend who built a large Network Marketing income. Her and her husband were earning over $50k a month. That company only paid them once a month. You may be shocked to know that every month they were counting down the days until their commissions were paid. They spent every last dollar of that $50k month after month. ***Learning to manage your finances NOW will go a long way as you build your residual life. Before long your ability to not only influence others, but to actually help and advise them will continue to grow.***

Would others say that you are confident or insecure? Confidence goes a long way when it comes to influencing others. I cannot think of one person that feels good about following someone who is unsure. Certainty is a big part of building trust in others. I will never forget the day after I signed up in my first Network Marketing company. Myself and a co-worker friend of mine had not only talked about the girl that would-be my enroller and her repeated attempts to enroll me in her business, but we laughed about it. I knew I was going to be under the same scrutiny and criticism as soon as I announced that I had tasted the proverbial kool-aid. On that day, I came in the salon with a secret, and it gave me a spring in my step. I was excited about my future and I had a plan! My friend knew me and could tell something was up. She asked me, "What's going on?" I insisted it was nothing, but she could tell I was holding something back. She knew I was excited about something.

> **" Having confidence is a result of personal development, a willingness to be coached and having the courage to step out and do the 'scary' things "**

So finally I couldn't hold back and said, "Well you're going to laugh at me, but I signed up with my client in a Network Marketing company, and I am going to quit this job in six months". I made that statement with certainty, because I knew that I was going to make it work come hell or high water. I was expecting her to poke fun at me. I was certain I was about to hear the same ridicule from her that I had dished out. Much to my surprise her response was, "Well I want to do it too!" What?! I was shocked. This was a BIG lesson for me. Because of my confidence and my certainty about where I was going, she felt safe enough to borrow it and jump in too. We also call this posturing. ***Confidence is sexy and people are attracted to it***. It allows people to feel safe in their uncertainty, knowing that if they hitch their wagons to someone confident, they are less likely to fail. I will spend more time about this in a later chapter discussing belief. Belief is a huge factor in becoming a more confident person, and in turn having a larger influence. Having confidence is a result of personal development, a willingness to be coached and having the courage to step out and do the 'scary' things. Here's the good news if you are not bursting with confidence yet. You get to hitch YOUR wagon to your confident and competent upline or enroller. You get to borrow their confidence, try it on and wear it around as you are building your team. You may not be confident in who YOU are yet, but you can certainly be confident in who THEY are, and that in turn will rub off and make you more confident as a result. Make sense? Part of my own confidence is because I have had a number of failures and really crappy things happen in my life and my network marketing career, and yet I am still here. I have been knocked down many times, and I've stood up and tried again. I have asked big bold questions and sometimes I get big bold answers. Sometimes I don't, but neither one killed me. So ultimately there is no reason to stand in fear or feel inferior to anyone or anything. Colin James says, "If it is possible in the world, it is possible for me, it is just a matter of how".

I am going to spend an entire upcoming chapter on the subject 'Becoming a Walking Billboard', because it is so important. This is another very powerful way to grow your influence and gain a lot of credibility. John Maxwell says that "Leadership is influence". That means that influence is leadership. All leadership starts by first leading yourself. Once you have successfully been able to lead yourself, your choices and your own life, then you will organically become a person who influences others. Your life is your biggest and most powerful example. Live it in such a way that people can't help but want to be around you. That is influence.

> " *Once you have successfully been able to lead yourself, your choices and your own life, then you will organically become a person who influences others* "

Shaking Hands & Kissing Babies

Chapter 5

"If you want to gather honey, don't kick over the beehive."
– Dale Carnegie

*T*he power of Network Marketing is in the power of your network and your ability to network with others. Before the massive presence of technology and Social Media, networking with others was the focus of Network Marketing. What I have noticed over the last 5 years or so is that there is a lot more marketing and a lot less networking. I am going to share some of my top tips for becoming a magnetic NETWORKER. No matter what profession you are in, you will always benefit from getting really good at how to network with others. Genuinely connecting with other human beings is a skill and a gift. No matter what your personality type, you can learn the skills, practice them over and over and become a master.

I want to first share a book with you. Dale Carnegie's 'How To Win Friends And Influence People'. It was copyrighted in 1936 yet the principals have stood the test of time. I love that book! I have read it more than once and I always recommend it to others. That book will help you to develop some very effective people skills. Some people are just born with them. They naturally have the ability to be 'likable' and 'memorable'. We live in a VERY busy world. People never have enough time. We use technology to fill in the gaps like texting and tweeting. We post and share things on our 'stories' and 'walls', pretending that Social Media is how we talk to others. I have three kids. They grew up in the age where cell phones, text messaging and Social Media were being born and became a primary means of communication. They were the first generation that could communicate almost solely with people via technology. People skills have suffered because of it. There are far less personal interactions and more technological interactions. As a Mom, I want nothing more than to hear my kids voices and have a quick chat with them, but they would much rather send me a text. The art of having an in-depth, interesting conversation is becoming less and less common. ***We almost need to take a step backward and re- learn how to become a person with GREAT people and communication skills***. Doing that will give you a major advantage in building your team, and in many other areas of your life.

I want to help you to become the person everyone wants

to know and be friends with. It always starts with how you present yourself. Are you approachable? Do you have a smile on your face? When I enter a room, I take a quick scan. Who is standing alone with their arms crossed? Who is standing in little 'clicks', only socializing with each other. Who is smiling and talking to everyone? THAT is the person I want to meet. I want to connect with the most friendly and connected person in the room. I love it when I meet someone new and we begin asking each other questions. A true Networker will do anything they can to add value to me. They will introduce me to someone that I 'Just have to meet', or someone who needs to meet me. Part of how you present yourself is how you are dressed. You don't need $200 jeans or designer clothes to look great. I have always noticed that when I feel good about my appearance, I feel more confident. You've heard the 'Dress to impress' line, right? Well I do that, but I am really only trying to impress ME. Make sure YOU feel good and confident about yourself. Your best accessory is your smile so wear it well. Look people in the eye and let your eyes smile as much as your mouth.

TIP: Practice having a smile on your face when you enter a room, it will not only make you more approachable, but it will make others feel at ease and excited to meet you.

Are you interesting or are you interested? Nothing makes people feel more valued or important than talking about themselves to someone else who is genuinely interested in them. Nothing will kill a conversation or a new friendship faster than dominating conversations by talking about yourself. I love to ask people questions and find out WHO they really are. This was a skill I brought with me into my Network Marketing profession. As a stylist, I got GREAT at asking questions to my customers all day long. I had their undivided attention for at least 2 hours at a time. Part of developing a relationship with them was really getting to know them, not just do a great job on their hair. People love to talk about themselves by sharing their knowledge or feeling like you are interested in what they are saying. Phase one of learning to be a GREAT Networker is getting great at asking questions, and then really listening to their responses. I am taking mental notes while someone is talking so I can be sure to remember important details about them, and how I can add value to their lives. Here are a few things you can ask when getting to know someone new:

- What do you do for a living?
- How did you get into that?
- You must LOVE it!?
- Are you married?
- Do you have children?
- What do you do for fun?
- What are you the most passionate about?

One of my favorite things to ask in regard to someone's job/career. Do you LOVE it? This always elicits an interesting response. If they love it, their eyes will light up and they will share their excitement with you. Or, if they don't LOVE it, they will share with you all of the reasons why they don't. Take note of this because these are their current areas of dissatisfaction. *As a Network Marketing professional, finding out someone's pain points and areas of dissatisfaction can be KEY points for you in discussing potential new OPTIONS for them.* Find the need and fill it. Find your new friend's needs and fill them with your solutions. Get great at active listening. Listen for what is NOT being said, what is implied and what emotions are created when they are talking to you. Your goal does NOT have to be offering your solution right then and there if it's not the natural progression of that conversation. Maybe for this initial talk, you are just getting to know each other with NO agenda. Too many Network Marketers go in for the KILL ... oops, I mean for the 'sale' too soon, and it can feel desperate and cause people to feel pressured. One thing you need to always remember is that this is a relationship business. Therefore, the relationship should always come first. People sign up for one reason and they stick around for another. Without legitimate relationships with people on the team, it is easy for them to leave. However, if they feel connected to and empowered by a community, and if they feel part of a tribe, they will not only stick around, they will stay engaged and be a contributing member of the group. Take a genuine interest in other people's lives and you will gain a lifelong relationship.

TIP: Develop genuine relationships with people with NO benefit to you, build solid relationships.

Are you a giver or a taker? When it comes to connecting, you want to be a GIVER! You know, the person in any room that knows everyone and connects people who can add value to others lives. I recently joined my local Chamber of Commerce. I have been a member many times over the years on and off, and I think getting involved with your own local community is an incredible way to connect. I attended my first business mixer shortly after becoming a member. I walked up to the event alone. I introduced myself to the people at the check in table and walked in with a smile on my face. Shortly thereafter I was greeted by a Chamber Ambassador. He was a very friendly, energetic guy. He asked me all about why I was there, and what I did. I in turn asked him a number of questions. As a result of our conversation, he walked me around and introduced me to several people he thought I could add value to, or who could add value to me. It was a fun event and I met a lot of new people. As a result of that event I met a new business partner. The Chamber Ambassador I met was so charged by our conversation and the questions I asked him, he ended up quitting his job and pursuing his dream. He alone connected me with almost a dozen new 'friends'. I do my best to figure out a way that I can GIVE to people right away. How can I add value to their lives, or their business? Who can I connect them with that will help them move forward? How can I help this person? I know that if I can become a connector, an encourager or a friend, or add any type of value to them, they will remember me. I am essentially putting pennies in our relationship piggy bank. I keep adding and adding as much and as often as I can. I want to fill up the piggy bank so one day I can make a withdrawal. I am building up credibility, and I am developing a relationship of trust and friendship. If and when the time comes for me to talk with them about what I do in my business, they are excited to be involved with me! They know I am not only trying to serve myself, but that I am looking out for them too. They now trust me because I have already showed them that I care about them, and what is important to them. This is a valuable lesson about reaping and sowing. If you are never sowing seeds of friendship or adding value and connecting, you will never have a harvest to reap.

Getting involved.

I am the first to admit, it is EASY to be uninvolved. I have two adult kids who are grown and living on their own, and one teenager left at home. The days of being super busy with kids activities and events is over for me now. I work at home. Technology has made it easy to get things done from my cell phone or laptop. I can buy groceries from home, shop for just about anything from my phone and many of the errands we used to have to drive around to finish, can be done via Wi-Fi and a device. It is so easy to be uninvolved, but if pursuing a residual life is your goal, then you need to leave your house. Get out and join a new gym or Church group. Volunteer somewhere, take a class or join your local Chamber. You need to get out and get active! Go have fun with friends, do play dates, lunch dates, or anything you can to get out and around other people. Host fun events at your house! Say YES more when you get invited to events or gatherings. I know some people who have packed social schedules, and guess what, they do great in Network Marketing! This can be something really fun! When people ask me what they should do to meet new people, I ask them what they LIKE to do? Maybe you have always wanted to take a cooking class. Well go do that! Maybe you want to learn to dance. Then go do it! It doesn't matter what it is, just go do it. ***Remember, if you feel your network is weak, you need to go build a new one.*** Trust me, people will not be knocking down your door to join your business. There are so many people that NEED what you have, and your job is to go find them. I will devote an entire chapter to Social Media later in the book, but if you meet people through Social Media, the goal is to as quickly as possible take it offline and develop that relationship. These skills are very important. Use your little adventures as training ground for talking to people, asking questions and adding value. Don't go in with the intention of getting people 'signed up'. Have the intention of making some great connections. Connections become friends. Friends can become business partners.

Following up.

When I meet new people, I do my best to follow up with them in 24 hours. I want them to add me to their contacts and remember me. I send a text or email right away and just say thank you for the conversation and connection. I can say that I am always so impressed and grateful to receive a follow up note or message when I meet someone. It feels like they went the extra mile, and that makes me feel important. Our goal should always be to make people feel important. The sad fact is that most people never follow up. In Network Marketing follow up is a secret weapon. Think of it like this; maybe your friend has already heard about your product or company. Maybe they even know someone who is already using and/or selling it, but they never followed up. Then you walk into the picture. You are excited and you are adding value to their lives. You make them feel important and YOU follow up. That other person literally laid the groundwork, but you will reap the rewards because you took the time to follow up. Always remember this can work the other way too, if you fail to follow up. You will just be paving the way for someone else to earn the reward for your hard work. Don't make it that easy for people. Follow up, follow up and then follow up again. Our current enroller followed up with Bobby for six years. Yes, six years! Was it worth the six year wait for him? YES of course it was!

We doubled his income in less than 2 years. If you don't follow up, you are leaving money on the table. Jim Rohn said, "The fortune is in the follow up". He was right! It is a key skill to becoming a great Networker and in building a massive team.

TIP: Follow up is a secret weapon. Low tech, high touch, or high tech high touch; make people feel valued by following up, and keep doing it until the timing is right for them whether it's 6 weeks or 6 years.

Finally, I want you to paint a picture of the perfect networking relationship. When you can create a win/win partnership, *this is the sweet spot.* This is when both you and the other person are gaining something from the meetup or new friendship. If it is a one-sided relationship, over time it will fade away. I have done business with many different people over the years. I am a loyal client and always do my best to help them build their brand or business through referrals or recommendations to others. I have a friend in the health and wellness world whom I had referred dozens and dozens of people. I had faithfully referred new people who became long term clients year after year for her. A couple of times over the years I invited her to partner with me, so she could in turn refer clients to me. I proved many times over through the years that I was very interested in helping her just for the sake of helping her, with nothing at all in it for me. I love to help other people who have a skill, product or service I love. After a few unsuccessful attempts to partner with her, I was left feeling that our relationship was one sided. She was only in the relationship for what I could give to her and had zero interest in reciprocating. I would much rather partner with someone who finds as much value in what I offer as I do in what they offer. This is a win/win relationship. We both stand to feel valued and appreciated. This has been a hard lesson for me to learn over the years. I hope to pass it on to you. In order to create an incredible reputation as a GREAT connector, you must continue to create relationships that are mutually beneficial for both of you.

" *In order to create an incredible reputation as a GREAT connector, you must continue to create relationships that are mutually beneficial for both of you* "

Bigger Belief

Chapter 6

*"Whether you believe you can do
a thing or not, you are right."
– Henry Ford*

We talk a LOT about belief in this profession.
There are truckloads of books, dozens of seminars, webinars, podcasts and classes you can take part in that are all designed to help you build your belief. It is a complex subject and very multi-facetted. First, there is belief in yourself. This one is deep. It goes back to childhood mindsets and attitudes that were passed on to you from your family, important people in your life and the belief systems you were raised in. Then there is belief in the profession of Network Marketing. To me, this one seems easier to develop. There are enough facts, figures and stories available to you that help you develop a good solid belief in Network Marketing as a viable and credible profession to take part in. Just knowing there are SO MANY people who have chosen this profession, and that

have been able to create wild success is a pretty good clue. Next there is belief in your own company, products and compensation plan. This is another belief that is fairly simple to develop. I'll go into some of the steps you can take to build your belief in these areas.

The simple fact about belief is that whatever your belief is, that will be true for you. Your belief becomes a self-fulfilling prophecy for your life. If you woke up today believing that it would be an amazing day, chances are very likely that it will be exactly that... an AMAZING day! Belief is a very powerful force that is either working FOR you or AGAINST you. I want to help you grow your belief so you will feel ten feet tall and bulletproof.

Fact: The higher your level of belief is, the more believable you become to others.

Belief is this intangible thing that will ooze out of you when you are interacting with others whether you are conscious of it or not. When you lack belief in any area, inadvertently people sense it. This is why it is important to work on developing a strong belief in these specific areas.

Let's start with you. Your belief in yourself, your abilities and skills or talents. I want you to know this from the start. No matter where you have come from, YOU CAN DEVELOP THE SKILLS IT TAKES TO BUILD A HUGE Network Marketing BUSINESS! This is not an opinion, it is a fact. If you want it bad enough you will work to learn and develop the skills it takes until to reach your goal.

Fact: Belief grows stronger when you are in action /activity.

Make sure to align yourself with a mentor/coach that believes in you. You can use THEIR belief in you while you are growing your own. You may not believe YOU can do it, but if you believe THEY can do it, all you have to do is borrow their belief and trust in their skills.

TIP: Mentorship + Actions = Belief

If your emotions and feelings aren't there yet, make sure your actions are. Are you committed to being in activity? Are you committed to developing new habits? Are you allowing your mentor to coach you, or are you questioning them and giving excuses as to why you cannot follow their coaching? You may not think this is related to belief, but trust me when I say it is directly related to it. How can you have belief in yourself to learn a new career if you have not taken the time to learn it?

Let me give you an example. What if today you decided that you wanted to be a hairdresser. So tomorrow you go into a salon to work and you have 5 clients. You give all 5 of them haircuts. On day 2 you go and do the same thing again. If you gave those 10 people terrible haircuts would you walk away saying to yourself and others that hairdressing didn't work? Would you feel discouraged with your skills or lack thereof? Of course not! You never learned the skills it takes to do a great job at cutting hair! And you certainly haven't given it enough time to get better with practice.

The same is true of this profession. You cannot expect to be a ten out of ten with your personal belief if you never take the time to develop your skills. With every activity you are growing it more and more. And the beautiful part is, WHILE you are learning and developing skills, and while you are borrowing your belief from your mentor, you are still able to earn money and grow your business. This makes it 100 percent possible for ANYONE to have belief in themselves. Once you have reached the point where you are now the person who is pouring belief into someone else, you'll be able to speak from personal experience about how to make that happen. It's an incredible system that can be passed on again and again. The more activity you are in, the faster your belief will grow if you are following the guidance of a successful mentor/coach. Just like in my example of cutting hair, you must find someone who will show you the steps they took to be successful. You must put in the time and the effort. These steps cannot be skipped. While it may feel uncomfortable to be taking actions you're not familiar with or even skilled at, over time that will all change. ***Better skills = better results = bigger belief.***

TIP: The more business building activity you engage in, the faster your belief will grow.

Believing in the profession.

I gave you some valuable information about the profession in chapter one, but if you really want to feel confident in what this profession is, you can also do some of your own research. Here are a few agencies you can look up for statistics, history and the current status of the entire direct selling profession. One is *www.dsa.org* and the other is *www.wfdsa.org*. Both of these websites will offer you an array of information from current sales numbers to best practices for building a business and choosing a company. I belief that information allows for clarity, and clarity breeds belief. When you see the power and history of this incredibly large global profession, it gives you a sense of security in knowing that it's here to stay. It is a force in the world today, both for providing GREAT products and services, and also for providing incredible opportunities to generate income. I have read as many books as I could to teach me as much as possible about the profession that I love. For me, that information was so interesting and helpful in building a solid foundation of belief for me. No matter what someone else's 'opinion' is, I have done enough research and have enough knowledge that no one can shake my belief. No one can sway **what I know to be true**, which makes me feel ten feet tall and bulletproof! I am a ten out of ten with my belief in the profession!

Building belief for yourself in the company you choose can be as easy as attending a large corporate event. You will get to see and feel the culture in action. You will learn the story of the founders, and the products. You'll hear from top leaders and Corporate Executives. You will have the opportunity to meet other distributors, both brand new and seasoned pros. Your company should have a system and tools available for you. These tools should include both information and training on your products/services, and how to build a team. Getting familiar with the assets your company has to offer will build a lot of belief. Knowing they are doing their part in providing information and tools to you is huge. My recommendation to you is that you get to your company's next Corporate event ASAP and watch your levels of belief soar. I can just about guarantee that you'll move your belief needle in the right direction.

The entire next chapter is devoted to becoming a walking billboard. If you want to build your belief and believability in your company's product, then become your own best customer. Try everything. Use it intentionally. Fall madly in love with it. Organic passion will grow, and you will NOT be able to stop sharing your amazing experience!

How do you build belief in your company's compensation plan? What if you don't know the difference between yours and any other company's comp plan? What if you don't understand how it works? I am going to answer this for you in two phases.

Phase one.

Surprisingly, the vast majority of people involved in building a business in the Network Marketing profession rarely understand exactly how their compensation plan works. I am always shocked by this! This would never happen in a traditional job. You always know exactly what you're being paid, how you can make more and what you need to do to increase your paychecks. For some odd reason in this profession many people don't make it a priority to learn and understand how to get paid. I remember when I first got started, the compensation plan seemed complicated. There were many different facets to it, but because I LOVE numbers and I really wanted to understand how I was getting paid, I studied it. I read the long documents, watched the videos and scoured my commission checks until I fully understood how it worked, how I was getting paid and how I could maximize what was being offered. Most companies have a variety of ways for you to earn upfront bonuses, monthly incentives, trips, bonus pools and team/residual pay. If you don't take the time to learn it, or at the very least learn what is available, I can guarantee that you will be leaving money on the table. Hopefully your enroller/mentor understands your company's compensation plan and is paying attention to your business, as you are getting started. They can guide you through what it takes to earn and how NOT to miss out on commissions. If that person doesn't know it well enough to teach you, keep searching up the line of sponsorship until you find someone who can.

Your company will have videos and documents that you can watch and study to help you understand how you get paid, but the best way to learn it... start earning! Nothing will help you learn better and faster than doing the work, and then seeing your commissions posted with a weekly/monthly breakdown on a report from your company (Which most companies do now). This is also a big-time belief builder! If you happen to have an unsupportive spouse or partner, nothing will get them on board like some extra zeros in your commission. As a leader, you will need to know this information. You will need to keep a watchful eye on your new business partners to ensure they maximize their earnings, and so they don't miss out on any potential bonuses or commissions. This will continue to build your belief, and this will be a big factor in helping your business partners build their belief. They will see you as the leader and someone who is watching out for them, someone who is helping them to NOT miss out.

Phase two.

I am separating this next portion from the information

you just read. This part is not necessary for the average person, but if you are a leader, or if you are a more seasoned Network Marketer, this can be very valuable in building your belief and the belief of those on your team. As an experienced Network Marketing professional and being that I am married to a Network Marketing Guru, there are times when you may want to be able to know and explain the differences in various compensation plans. I have participated in three different plans. I owned a Network Marketing company and knew that compensation plan frontwards and backwards, and I have studied other plans from a variety of companies. Bobby has participated in a few more than me over the last 30 plus years so he has seen so many and really understands how they work.

" The more belief you have, the more believable you are "

Remember I said I love numbers? Well I certainly do, and I love to study and learn about how numbers are used in Network Marketing comp plans. Over the years there have been some very creative plans that's for sure, but not all of them have fit into legal parameters. Knowing how your company's compensation compares to others can be helpful. How it is better, where it is different and where it isn't as good. When you learn this for yourself, you will have an entire new level of belief in your own comp plan. Knowing the details of how any compensation plan works can ONLY help build your belief and the belief of your business partners. Knowing why someone may prefer one type of compensation over another can also be a powerful tool. My first company was an older one. It had a limited uni-level compensation plan with lots of party plan aspects to it. It was very hard for the average person to build a full time income. Bobby and I built with this plan to a six figure per year income in less than 6 months. BUT, once we had some new leaders emerging and rank advancing to the higher levels, our personal commissions WENT DOWN drastically! Yes, in that company, building leaders actually reduced your income. WHAT?! That was a hard reality to swallow. We should be motivated by our compensation to grow as many leaders as possible, not hinder them. Now when I talk with people about compensation, I have the experience to be able to guide people in the best direction for them. Again, this second phase is just bonus information for you. The most important thing for you is knowing YOUR compensation plan well enough to show it and teach it.

Belief is an important thing to have for a number of reasons. I said it earlier; the more belief you have, the more believable you are. When you feel ten feet tall and bulletproof in your own belief, people can see and feel it. It shows in the way you sound, your tone of voice, and your body language. ***When you are looking someone***

in the eye and speaking with some authority, your energy is higher and thus more attractive to them. The goal for you is to have unshakable belief. That will carry though and be transferred to your new team members, and help them while they are also growing their belief.

It is wildly important when you are speaking to new potential business partners. I mentioned posturing earlier. Let me add some clarity to this. Posturing for me in Network Marketing is not about presenting something that isn't true. Posturing is about the attitude you carry with you into your conversations with potential partners. Automatically people are drawn to confidence. They feel more trust with someone who is confident about what they are doing. To contrast this, if you yourself are uncertain about your products, your opportunity or even with yourself, people will feel fear in joining or following you. If you don't know where you are going, how can you help them figure out where they are going? They need to feel that YOU are the perfect person to help them reach their goals. If your belief waivers, then you cannot speak to others with authentic confidence about why THIS is the answer they have been praying for. Too many Network Marketers have an attitude of "Oh, I sure hope I GET this person!" That is a wrong way of thinking about it. Yes, the truth is, you need people to join your team, use and love your products, and also join the crusade of changing people's lives through your opportunity as well, BUT you don't 'GET' people. In this profession we partner with people. They need you, and you need them. It is a two-way street of need. This is a business of people helping other people fill the gaps and finding solutions.

" If your belief waivers, then you cannot speak to others with authentic confidence about why THIS is the answer they have been praying for "

Walking Billboard
Chapter 7

"You can't build a reputation on what you are GOING to do."
– Henry Ford

*H*ere is where the rubber meets the road. It really is pretty easy to talk about the things we should be doing or saying, and how we should be acting and responding, but actually DOING them is something altogether different. It is a lot harder to put your money where your mouth is. I feel like we have heard this our entire lives, yet still it is something we need to keep hearing. As a parent, I have been forced to be intentional about what I say and do. I have always tried (Not always successfully) to make sure that my words align with my actions. I wanted to build trust in my kids, knowing that I walked my own talk. This becomes an important character trait in Network Marketing. People are choosing YOU to align themselves with. They make that choice for a variety of reasons. There is a trifecta of traits that when they all come together at the same time, a YES is inevitable. Ok, here it is. ***When someone KNOWS you, LIKES you and TRUSTS you***, and when that happens at the same time, people will be confident, comfortable and excited about partnering with YOU!

TIP: Be your own biggest and best customer.

In an earlier chapter, I briefly mentioned that becoming a walking billboard would have a BIG impact on your level of influence. Here is why that is very important. If you happen to be someone who has a small circle of influence, it can take time to do the things you will need to do to raise it. The fastest way to grow your current level of influence, regardless of where you are starting, is to become a walking, talking advertisement for your company's products or services. Some results are more visible than others. If you are in the health and wellness category of Network Marketing, then having a physical transformation is KEY. You may have never had success in business or have never made a significant amount of money. You may have never had any credibility before, but transform your body and everyone will take notice. All of a sudden you are now the credible person to help and give advice to others. It is a remarkably powerful tool that you have 100% control over. Any product that allows you to LOOK physically different to the people who see you everyday, WILL help you grow your influence. That is why it becomes not just a good idea, but a requirement in building a business. So be your biggest and best customer and watch your credibility soar. Bobby and I started to build our business with the usual methods. We reached out to people and shared our crusade and vision for the future. We would cast a vision for them and invite them to join us on the journey. We did have a certain level of success, but when we visually transformed our bodies and allowed people to see the journey, we couldn't stop people from joining us. They could see with their own eyes that something was working. I feel that your own personal testimony and transformation are far more powerful than the ones you use from other people within your company or your team. ***The people in your circle know YOU, so seeing changes in YOU has the most influence.*** Make using your products or services your job. Even people we had reached out to about our opportunity reached back out to us to ask what we were doing to get such incredible results. On the flip side of this, I had a good friend who was a top leader in a skincare and cosmetics company. She didn't even use her own products! When people asked her about certain products, she could never give a complete or even truthful answer. Privately she told me how she liked other products better or couldn't use her own products for various reasons. Let me just tell you, people can feel the difference between a sales person and an authentic believer. Eventually this girl ended up changing companies over and over. I believe it has a lot to do with the fact that she never fully allowed herself to experience the benefits of becoming her own best customer. Do yourself and your business a favor and get AMAZING results with your products! Fall in love with them! Your authentic experience is more valuable than any sales pitch could ever be.

The concept of walking the talk goes deeper than just your products. People are more informed than ever before in history. We have obscene amounts of information available within seconds to us. We have seen so many things in the media over the years and people are savvy as consumers, and in assessing other people. We live our lives on blast now. Social media has created a world in which we show so much of ourselves and our lives to others. Being real and authentic, although it may seem rare, is so important because it is easier than ever to sniff out fakes.

Network Marketing is and always will be a relationship business. The people in my business become my family. We walk through life together both inside and outside of the business. Being a person that walks their own talk matters.

" Being a person that walks their own talk matters "

If you are talking about generosity and giving back,

but you never take actions that are congruent with that message, people will eventually notice. If you speak of having grace for others and meeting people where they are at, but you are hard-hearted, never forgive others when they make mistakes or you make people feel bad for where they are in their current season, people will begin to see things in you and realize you are not who they thought you were. Bobby has always said this to me, ***"Time will either promote you or it will expose you."*** This is so powerful and true! I had a person on my team who told me I was fake. I will call her Brenda. She told me that I was not the person I 'pretended' to be. Brenda knew that there was another member of the team, I will call her Barb, who had behaved in ways that needed a little correction. In an attempt to help Barb, I had a conversation with her as a friend, and offered some perspective. I wanted the very best for Barb. I knew first hand that we are all on a journey and that this could be a lesson that would help her grow. After our conversation, I continued to love and support Barb whether she took my coaching to heart or not. Meet people where they are at right? Brenda did not like my choices AT ALL. She saw my actions as fake. She saw grace as phony. It took a few months before Brenda saw that my actions were authentic and that I genuinely cared for Barb. People make mistakes sometimes whether they are big or small. I know that and I've made big and small mistakes myself. My only hope is to only make THOSE mistakes once; learn from them, get better, and grow. I offer this same grace to anyone I am around. This was a completely foreign concept to Brenda. She saw it as weak or even fake. Once she realized it was in fact real grace or an act of love toward Barb, she changed her tune. I was no longer fake, but a great person in her eyes. Time had promoted me.

Being a person whose actions are congruent with their character takes self-discipline. Certainly we all have emotions and may want to react with emotion sometimes, but learning to respond instead of reacting will take you a long ways.

TIP: You cannot take people on a journey you have not been on yourself.

Walk your talk as a leader in Network Marketing. You cannot teach and train people to do things that you are not doing or haven't done yourself to create success in your Network Marketing business. We are not anyone's boss in this profession, but we are partners. We can only guide and coach people to take the actions that we have taken to be successful ourselves. If your team knows that you are telling them to do things you are not doing, or that you have not done, they will begin to resent your coaching. As your business begins to grow and you have more leaders, there may be certain things that you no longer have to do, but you will continue to teach to your team so you can to help them reach the levels of success that you have reached. This is normal. I had a friend who was on my team who accused me of telling people to do things I wasn't doing myself. I explained to her that at her current level of success in the business, she would need to take certain actions to reach the next level. I was not currently taking those actions, however, I had been for many years, and I was reaping the rewards from those actions. I never teach or train on something I have not had experience with. *I will only pass down information I can confidently say that does and will result in success because I have tested it myself.*

I believe that a person's intentions expresses itself in energy. That is why sometimes you don't know why, but you just have a bad feeling about someone. Or the opposite can be true. You may have no real reason, but you just like someone and feel like they are a good person. Over time a person who has less than upright intentions, can no longer hide who they really are. There may be little signs along the way, but over time they all add up and the truth is revealed. I think this is partially why some people have a bad taste in their mouths about Network Marketing. They may have aligned with someone who didn't really care about them or their success. Their true intention was self motivated. They didn't really care to help you succeed, and only wanted to create more for themselves. Sadly, people can sometimes make an assumption about the profession as a whole because of that experience. However, when you align yourself with a heart centered leader; one who makes your goals THEIR goal, you will have a different experience altogether. Let me be clear on something. There is NOTH-ING wrong with being motivated to create your own success. That is why most of us begin this journey. We have dreams for ourselves and our future. It gets sticky when your personal desires impede your ability to serve and coach those on your team. I'll share more about this in the chapter on leadership.

You must become a person who takes action. Follow your own best advice. Over the years I have heard Bobby say over and over, "Would you want to enroll YOU today based on your actions". He has challenged people to duplicate their very best efforts every day. This is a simple way to hold yourself accountable and to a higher standard of activity. Take action on that lesson as soon as possible. Do not wait. Your actions will inspire many more people than your words.

TIP: Watching you succeed will build massive belief in your team.

People want to connect with and feel something real. Since leading in this profession is a matter of character, being a person of integrity and walking your talk is part of how to become a leader worth following. A walking billboard can look like this:

- Being your own best customer.
- Personally enrolling new people on a regular

basis.

- Developing new emerging leaders on a regular basis.
- Showing up to team calls and events.
- Being engaged with your team regularly via calls, social media pages and events.
- Meeting people where they are within their journey.
- Showing encouragement.
- Putting people and relationships before the business.
- Always telling the truth with love and compassion.
- Leading by example in life and in business.

Network Marketing leaders can be some of the best people you'll ever meet. They are deeply engaged regularly in personal development. They are introspective and always working to become the best version of themselves that they can be. They work on relationships to make them healthy and whole. They have healthy boundaries. They are intentional about their health. They are disciplined. They are generous. They are great connectors. They are kind and encouraging. They are grateful. They have a servant's heart. They love to see others succeed. They stand for contribution and giving back. Becoming a walking billboard is a journey with no destination. If you continue to work to become the type of person worthy of being followed by others, your life will change in miraculous ways while you are building your legacy.

" If you continue to work to become the type of person worthy of being followed by others, your life will change in miraculous ways while you are building your legacy "

What It Takes
Chapter 8

"Always bear in mind that your own resolution to succeed is more important than any other."
– Abraham Lincoln

I am going to give it to you straight with no fluff. In your first year in this profession, you are going to want to quit more than once. Maybe even ten times! This isn't abnormal. This is part of the journey. If you make it through your first year and never felt like quitting, then you are different than most people, and I would guess you didn't really engage. There WILL come a time when you want to throw in the towel. But if you **really desire the freedom** that comes from successfully building your Network Marketing empire, you will need to decide NOW that you are in this for the long haul. I am about to give you some specifics of what it takes to earn six figures a year in this profession. Now, I am not arrogant enough to think MY ways are the only ways, but what I have done works! Bobby has always said, "Everything works, just not all the time, and not for everyone". Meaning, you never know which video, which Social Media post, which website, which opportunity call, which event etc. is going to grab somebody's attention. You can't possibly know when timing will be right for your prospect. Use ALL of them! It is a matter of consistently getting information to as many people as possible, and doing it over and over again until the timing is right for them. I am going to tell you what I have done three separate times to grow my Network Marketing business to six figures as fast as possible.

Decide.

Be committed to 12 months of consistent action as your first target. It is incredibly important to understand that this takes time. You have to give yourself enough time to learn and develop skills. Far too many people quit far too soon. ***Don't be one of them***. Talk to your family, and share with them the vision you have for them and your commitment to get it done. Get 'buy in' from them to help keep you accountable and to support you on your journey. When I joined my first Network Marketing company, life was already busy. I worked in the salon 50 to 60 hours a week, and Bobby owned a mortgage company. My oldest daughter was a freshman in high school, my son was in middle school and our baby girl went to daycare. On any given day we were all off in five different directions. Life was going very fast! Once I made the decision to go for it, Bobby and I sat the kids down and had a family meeting. We said, "We know that everyone is very busy right now, but it is going to get even busier. We are going to be gone even more than we are now. But the goal is that in 6 months, Mom & Dad will be home twice as much. We are going to need your help. You'll be heating up more frozen pizza for dinner, and getting less help with homework. We are going to need more help with the baby and with the chores. But if we all can stick it out, everyone's lives will be better." We painted a picture of WHY we were going to have an ever harder, busier life than we already did. We wanted them to know that it wouldn't last forever though. It was only for a season, and it would be worth it for them and for us. We shared a six-month timeline with them and thanked them for doing this WITH us.

TIP: Share the vision with your family of how this will benefit all of them, so that you can get their support.

Why. I had very emotional reasons why each time I began building. I had a fiery sense of urgency! I believe that grit is born from the kind of **WHY** that is wrapped around a financial need. I believe grit is born when your need is big and urgent. I share this with you a second time because YOU need to identify and know this for your own journey. You need to dig deep and feel the emotion behind the actions you will be taking. I have yet to meet a top leader who began their journey with no need. In fact, many were in dire situations. Most needed a change and needed it quick. In my case, I was desperate! I needed to make things happen for my family and it needed to happen fast. That drove me to take **massive** action. It drove me past fears and insecurities. The need, the why, was bigger than any and all reasons I had to slow down, stop or quit. I think it was actually a blessing that my need was so prevalent. I was in a do or die situation which left me with one option... make this work at all costs!

Building the tribe.

"Never underestimate the power of a small group of committed people to change the world. In fact, it is the only thing that ever has." – Margaret Mead

I began actively seeking out people I could partner with right away. I knew that I needed to begin finding people who wanted to change their lives as well. I am constantly asked if I lead with the opportunity or the products. My answer to that is YES. I lead with both. One does not exist without the other. But truth be told, I lead my conversations with VISION. I cast a vision for people of the future **they desire**. How do I know what that is? I ask a LOT of questions. Once I know the future they desire, I begin to paint a detailed picture of how that can become a reality. Finding customers to use your products is very easy. If you have products that work great, and I am assuming you do, then people are going to want to use them. Finding business partners is a little more challenging. But one committed business partner can bring you hundreds and maybe even thousands of new customers. It takes exactly the same amount of effort and words to cast a vision of a better life as it does to share a great product testimonial. I have never been a monster enroller, but what I am great at is finding people who catch the vision. ***I am always strategically looking for partners***. Once I find them, it is GO time! Each time I began a build over the years, it was about urgency. How much activity could I compress into small pockets of time I had in my days. What does that activity look like? For me it always starts with your immediate circle. I help people to talk to those in their circle of friends and family immediately. Before you get weird on me ... It is a very natural thing to talk to them first. If you opened a traditional brick and mortar business, hopefully these would be the people that would know all about it long before you held your grand opening. It is actually unnatural to avoid talking to them. Next, I help them schedule events in their home or one on one get togethers within their first 14 days. My goal is to get my new partner paid their first commission as quickly as I can. There is something magical about that very first commission. It makes it real! It builds belief, and has magic fairy dust all over it. I know that the faster I can get them paid, the more excitement that it will create.

TIP: Focus on getting your new business partner paid as quickly as possible to help build their excitement and belief.

Another thing I have learned over the years is that my success grows exponentially when I have personally enrolled new people in groups or blocks. Initially there was nothing strategic or intentional about it. I had my head down, and I was going as hard as I could. There wasn't a lot of strategy involved. Years later I was at an exclusive leadership event when I heard Eric Worre talk about his strategy of enrolling 20 people in 30 days. It was a lightbulb moment for me. As I looked back at what I had built over the years, that theory held true. Any residuals I had built could be traced back to surges or blocks of people being enrolled by Bobby and I in compressed periods of time. You could have enrolled the exact same number of people as I did over a 12 month period and have very little energy or results. But enroll 20 people in 30 or 45 days and boy oh boy, the energy is high and the chance for big things happening is huge! Now that I am aware of the impact of enrolling a lot of people in short blocks of time, I train people to understand that if they are wanting to really kick start their business, they need to go on an enrolling spree. You may be wondering how can I control this? You cannot predict if or when someone will say yes right? That is 100 percent true; you certainly can't. You can however control the amount of people you are contacting and connecting with daily. After all it is a numbers game, and numbers never lie. If you want to personally enroll ten people this month, you will most likely have to have 50 or more real conversations. There are always exceptions to these numbers but over time they are pretty accurate. The numbers will vary but as your skills get better, the number of people you enroll will improve.

How many names do you need to have on your **oh so important prospecting list**? A Lot! Over time, you will need to accumulate hundreds and hundreds of names. I want you to know that dipping your toe into this business will not get you very far. You need to dive in and get busy. Your mentor will be with you every step of the way. It is one of their main priorities. A while back I enrolled a girl, who enrolled another girl, and they both enrolled at the same time. The girl enrolled by my prospect was HUNGRY to succeed! She used $200 of the last $250 she had in her bank account to sign up. She caught the vision and wanted to know how fast she could earn that money back. I walked her through the first few steps, and off she went. She did a post on a Social Media platform and showed a picture of her results after just a few days on the products. That post achieved crazy attention! I informed her how to respond to each person who commented, and that her goal was to take those comments off line and into a live 3-way conversation with me. For 5 days straight she had me booked on 3 way calls every 15 – 20 minutes. I had never done so many calls before with one person in my career. Many things happened as a result of this ***massive action***. First, she got a handful of new enrollments! This is a big deal because it was ALL cold market. She didn't know any of the people who responded to the post. Second, over the course of those 5 days, she took 15 pages of notes during the conversations we had. It was like a crash course in prospecting and a perfect training opportunity for her. She earned back her investment and did very well at the start of her business. Remember, enrolling one or two people over long periods of time just won't get it done. Yes, it is great to be a consistent enroller, and it is great to have personal enrollment goals every month, but if you are looking for explosive energy on your team, it starts with you and the amount of new energy YOU can create by enrolling a larger number of people all at the same time.

TIP: Compress as much energy and as many enrollments into a short period of time to create massive energy.

I am 100 percent willing to be anywhere at any time for a new partner. They get my absolute full attention. If they live two hours away and have people who want to meet with me twice a week, I drive the miles and show up. My goal is to find the most excited, most influential person in the room. That can only happen if I am IN the room with them. I connect with as many people as I can so I can start creating new relationships. I am looking for the visionaries and the runners, and once I find them, we run! I personally enrolled another girl, who enrolled a girl that was very excited and had a lot of influence. She lived a little more than 80 miles from me, and WOW was she making things happen! I drove to her house and the homes of other newly enrolled people on her team two to three times a week for at least six months. (Maybe that doesn't seem like a big deal to you, especially if you commute every day for work.) These in-home presentations were all held in the evening. I live in Southern California so I have one word for you, TRAFFIC! It would sometimes take me two and a half hours, one-way, to reach my destination. I drove each mile with a smile on my face knowing I was building an amazing future for myself and my family, and helping to add fuel to the fire burning on this expanding new team! My efforts with that excited group of people were a major contributor in growing our business to six figures in nine months. The return on the investment of all that driving, and hours away from my family doing presentations was far greater than the consistent effort it took to create it. ***Sadly, so many people just don't seem to be willing to put in this type of effort.*** For the vast majority of people, they begin their Network Marketing career with a full-time job and a very busy life. I get it, I did too. I worked on my feet for 10 to 12 hours a day when I began. I had a toddler and two teenagers at home. I was about as busy as you can be. And yet, I made sure that in the evening, I was in someone else's home sharing with them the vision of a better future as many times a week as I could be. You need to be willing to put in a lot of concentrated effort for a period of time. How long? That depends on too many factors to give you a perfect answer. It depends on the pocket of people you find. It depends on the level of influence the people you meet possess. It depends on the sense of urgency that you build with. It depends on the amount of discomfort you're willing to live with while you get this thing done. Your ability to succeed will be directly related to your ability to be uncomfortable and to manage the unknown.

Sound hard? Let me tell you something … **YOU WERE MADE FOR HARD THINGS**! Pushing past what feels comfortable, and making your life harder for a season, will allow you to live with freedom and choices for a lifetime. We have bought into a big fat lie that if it doesn't feel good, we're not supposed to do it. Really? Go read any biography of an elite world class athlete and ask them if their daily regimen of training felt good. Go speak to the CEO of any Fortune 500 company and ask them if their journey was simple and without pain? Go to the gym and try to build some muscles, IT HURTS! The only way to grow a muscle is to tear it down first. It's in the healing of that broken down muscle where the growth happens. Do not kid yourself into thinking that building a six-figure residual income is going to be easy or feel good all the time. I hated being away from my family. I hated being gone all day and getting home when everyone was asleep. I hated missing out on things. But it was all worth it when I got to be home all day, and when

I got to have more choices because of the income I had created. How uncomfortable are you willing to get, and for how long are you willing to do it to be able to achieve this type of freedom?

Sacrifice.

In the urgency of my quest to get out from under my current situation, I didn't have time to wait around for people who weren't ready. Looking back this was a huge blessing. I was laser focused on my goal and it was all I thought about. There was no balance in my life. When people said "NO" to me, I wasn't even phased. If people didn't want to engage in activity with me, I didn't think twice about it. I was busy looking for the next person ready to engage on a journey of freedom with me. Maybe the next person would be my new partner, and maybe not, but I never made people feel less than, because of their choice. I just didn't have time to wait around for them. I kept moving. I realized very quickly that some things had to be removed from my life. I was not going to be able to build my business fast enough if I didn't make some space for it. What are you willing to give up temporarily to make this happen? This is HARD for some people. They just don't want to give up anything. They want to keep their lives as comfortable as possible. They don't want to give up TV, or game night or sports or kids activities, AHHHHH! UH OH!! Yes that is what I said. I have seen more incredible people throw away what could have been a MASSIVE business because they were not willing to make space in their lives. Sometimes great success may require great sacrifice first. Why is that so hard? I believe it is a powerful and beautiful message to teach your family. After all, you are all in it together. Allow them to participate in the journey, then when you reach your goals, the impact will be even more valuable and powerful for everyone. My kids had to sacrifice. They had to help out a lot. They had to step up and do things they didn't normally do. They didn't always love it, and neither did I. Recently I was having a conversation with a young man who was 22 years old. He is an aspiring music producer, and he really does possess some talent. In our conversation I made a few suggestions to him. One of them was getting a job at a music label and making some great connections so he could get his foot in the door. (aka networking) His response still bothers me. He told me he wasn't willing to start at the bottom. (Insert jaw drop here). How many people have given up on their dream because it was going to take too much time and effort to make it happen? Can I tell you something? My kids are the hardest workers. They all have an incredible work ethic, are driven, and they inspire me with who they have become as young adults. Just maybe a little of that came from them seeing that it takes hard work, sacrifice and commitment to reach goals. No matter what generation you come from, that message is timeless.

Sadly, many people have become addicted to the status quo. We have created comfortable lives that are much smaller than the ones we are supposed to be living. All in the name of safety, comfort and familiarity. The thing is, for many, a comfort zone isn't actually comfortable, it is just familiar. To build a six-figure income in your Network Marketing business you need to be uncomfortable for a while. You need to talk to people, often. You need to bravely share your WHY and your VISION. You need to ask questions and be bold. I often ask myself why more people aren't in this profession. I know the answer already. It isn't because it is hard and doesn't require anything specific to be a part of it. The downfall is that it takes real work, and that work is on top of all the other things going on in people lives. I am going to let you in on something. Once you have created a full-time residual income, you will wake up every day like you won the lottery. It is a lifestyle unlike what any other profession can provide. The sacrifices required to make this type of business happen are totally worth it, I PROMISE!

- Make room in your life for your business.
- For 12 months straight, be in massive recruiting mode.
- Make it a goal to be out sharing the presenta-

tion and vision at least two times a week.

• Be fully engaged and plugged in to anything your team and company have to offer.

• Grab an accountability partner or two to help keep you on track.

• Have a goal of getting at least 10 "NO's" a week.

• Take the time to train your new business partners - this will leverage your time and allow them to grow.

" The thing is, for many, a comfort zone isn't actually comfortable, it is just familiar "

Creating A Culture
Chapter 9

"Culture is like the wind. It is invisible; yet its effects can be seen and felt." – Bryan Walker

*F*inding a company with a culture that you can not only buy into but fall in love with is an important piece of the puzzle. When Bobby and I am were Co-Founders of our own Network Marketing company, we were very aware of the culture we wanted to create. The culture of a company is the beliefs, values, attitudes and the overall experience that people feel. When someone's core values don't line up with the culture of a company, they will eventually leave. If I am being totally transparent, I hadn't really put a ton of thought into the culture of a team until recently. I was on a call with the Global President of Sales and Marketing for a top 20 Global Network Marketing company. We were having an open discussion, and he commented back to me something that really caused me to think.

His comment was:

> *"The culture that Bobby and you had built on your team was rare, and that building a team culture was not only hard, not all leaders can do it."*

I couldn't disagree. I have always felt that our team has the best people on the planet, and they keep attracting more like-minded people. After that phone call, I really began thinking about how important it is to create a team culture as well as knowing how to do it. I have said this a few times already, but it is so important I am going to say it again. People sign up for one reason, but they stick around for another. A big part of that is the culture of the team.

Your team culture will begin with YOU! Who you are as a leader, as well as how you set the tone for everyone else. Because this profession predicates itself on a 'follow the leader' model; who you are, how you respond, train and treat your team will likely be duplicated. Your team will duplicate 100 percent of what you don't do, and 50 percent of what you do. Do you give a lot of recognition? How do you give it? Do you hold a lot of team events? Do you conduct training calls? Do you have team shirts? Do you have social media pages for you team? Do you have team social events? This is just a few examples, but these examples and many more will determine the type of culture that exists on your team. As your team grows, the culture will really begin to form.

Here are a few ways to lay the foundation for team culture.

Calls.

As soon as I jumped into Network Marketing, Bobby mentioned we needed to have a weekly call for team synergy and participation. Since he was my mentor and knew how to build teams, I listened and agreed. Every single week for the last 15 plus years, we have hosted team calls. On these calls we bring on emerging leaders from the team to allow them to be recognized and showcased in front of everyone else. We share testimonies, announce contests and incentives, promotions and announcements and good old fashioned Network Marketing 101 training. Bobby and I have always built together as a couple. We have different personalities, so our team would get a few different voices and perspectives on each call. We are also very playful, so our calls always have an element of fun. We love to laugh and make the business exciting! Having a weekly gathering of some sort is vital to creating and maintaining your team culture. It allows people to see others that are going through the same challenges and victories that they are. It helps people to feel that they are part of a community. It helps members of the team get to know each other better. We switched over to using the Zoom platform for our team calls a few years ago and it has been an awesome change to the way calls can be conducted. I love Zoom! Instead of just hearing voices, we can see each other's faces too!

Zoom has allowed us to build stronger bonds and deeper friendships. We get to see the look in someone's eyes and feel their passion through the screen. Technology is changing and improving so quickly that by the time you read this, we may be using something better!

Another benefit of having a weekly team call is the ability to help your leaders develop. Allowing more people to take part in the calls allows them to stretch, to learn how to communicate, and train more effectively.

> *" Having a weekly gathering of some sort is vital to creating and maintaining your team culture "*

Sometimes people are terrified of speaking on a call or at an event, so by having them participate more and more, they are developing the skills they will need in the future to lead their own teams. At first people will need a lot of direction and structure when speaking on a call, but little by little their skill will grow and before they know it they will be a pro and love doing it. I have seen it happen over and over through the years. Watching team members grow in their skill level is incredibly gratifying to see.

In addition to weekly team calls we have various other calls we do throughout the year. We do opt-in high accountability groups with our team which have their own private call once a week.

We have done leadership calls for anyone who have reached a certain rank. We have also done live opportunity calls over the years. Periodically we change things up so things don't get stale.

Recognition.

What and how do you recognize the people on your team? We use Social Media as a great way to show and share the recognition and milestones for our team members. I have found that a culture that celebrates as many things as possible is a very healthy one. By celebrating as many moments and achievements as you can, you are literally training the brain to succeed. We celebrate success with the products, new enrollments, personal breakthroughs, and any type of rank advancement. We celebrate when people take on more leadership, or have personal life victories outside of Network Marketing. We celebrate people joining the community. We celebrate just about anything we can! We use both public and private social media platforms to do this, as well as celebrate team members on live calls. We text and make phone calls to congratulate people when they reach goals. Recently a team member earned an incentive trip. She was not aware that she had qualified, so her enroller got a group of people on a call with her secretly. She didn't know any us were on the call. Then when he made the big announcement, we all cheered and shouted for her! It was such a magical emotional moment that we started doing it more often as a team. In most people's everyday lives, they rarely hear any encouragement or get recognized for a job well done. ***So coming into a community that celebrates you for so many things is so gratifying for people because they are having new life breathed into them.*** Who wouldn't want to be part of a community that is constantly building them up and cheering them on? Some people will work harder for recognition than they will for anything else.

Some teams have a culture of gift giving as part of recognition. I have mixed feelings about this. Yes, it is an incredibly thoughtful thing when someone takes the time to purchase and send you something for you hard work. However, because we live in a world of duplicable actions and activities, gift giving can create feelings of not being good enough and/ or not being able to keep up. If your enroller expresses congratulations via gifts, then that is what you in turn think you are supposed to do as your team begins to move up the ranks. Sometimes team members are just not in the position financially to be able to spend money in this way. It can create animosity within teams. People see others getting gifts, and if their enroller is not also doing that, they can begin feeling like they are on the wrong team. I actually had a girl quit my team because she saw another team giving a specific gift that I wasn't giving for a particular achievement.

Another reason I have mixed feelings is your company's compensation plan. If your company's compensation plan is a well-rounded one, it will have many ways for you and your team to earn commissions, gifts, rewards and vacations. You shouldn't have to ADD to it to incentivize your team, and if you teach your team that they need MORE than what your comp plan has to offer, then you are essentially de-edifying your own comp plan. You're telling your team that what your company offers isn't enough. If you want to build loyalty and trust in your company, you do not want to share the message that what they offer is NOT enough. Having special team contests and incentives is great, as long as it doesn't become the only reason your team decides to get into action.

TIP: Recognize people often and in front of others. This creates a culture of encouragement and celebration on the team.

System.

People cannot be duplicated, but systems can. What does it mean to have a system? A system is a specific set of procedures that your team follows with each and every new team member and customer. Having a system allows for anyone and everyone on your team to have the same chance at success, no matter who their enroller is. Sadly, people often get enrolled by someone who loses interest, quits or is also so new that they themselves don't know what to do to succeed. In most cases that person is left high and dry. I will always suggest that in this scenario you need to reach out to the company and find the next active person in your upline and connect with them. ***However, imagine if everyone on your team had access to the same information that is laid out in a very simple format with the exact steps they needed to take?*** A system empowers people to take action. A system gives people confidence, and empowers more belief because they don't feel the fear of the unknown. They know exactly what to do in order to have success.

We began implementing systems many years ago. Over the years they have evolved and become readily available to the entire team because of constantly advancing technology. If our goal for our teams is to create as much duplication as possible, we need to make sure that everyone is doing the same thing every time. As your team grows, this becomes harder and harder to accomplish. Have you ever played the telephone game? It is nearly impossible to get the information accurate after it goes through a handful of people. This same thing happens when building teams. That is why having a simple system for everyone to follow increases the amount of duplication that can happen. There is always a breakdown at some point. As soon as people start to make changes to the message, it gives others permission to make changes, and before long the original successful procedures have vaporized. If you do not have any type of system that you use for recruiting, getting a new person started and for leadership development, then you are missing out on what could be much faster team growth. Systems make building faster and easier. While it may take a little time to create one and get everyone on board using one, the benefits will be felt instantly, and the long-term rewards will inspire the entire team.

" It's not what works, it's what duplicates that matters "

When I first got started in my current company, I used the company presentation slides at all of my in-home presentations. Being the science-y dork that I am, I could talk science and statistics like no one else. I did a long and very informative presentation. I had an almost 100 percent sign up rate at my presentations. It was awesome! I was being asked to present more and more for our team because of all the enrollment success. Then one day I woke up and said, "Why am I doing so many of these?" "Why isn't my team stepping up to present the opportuntiy themselves"? Then it hit me! They couldn't do what I was doing. I had made it too complicated and hard. It was great information and people loved it, but it wasn't something that anyone but myself could effectively present. Remember what I said earlier in this book; It's not what works, it's what duplicates that matters. What I was doing was working, but it was not duplicating. Our goal should always be to leverage the tools and the leaders on our teams, and not just be THE ONE everyone needs. Right then and there I made a bold decision. I was going to totally revamp the presentation. *I was going to make it MUCH shorter and have an exact model for the team to follow that would allow ANYONE on the team to duplicate, no matter who it was.* At first the team was skeptical about this major shift. The presentation went from 52 slides to 11 and two short videos. There was only a very short amount of talking and the videos themselves were doing the bulk of the work. I believed it would work, but we needed to test it out on the team and see if it what we thought was true. I still remember the first time we presented it. A handful of leaders came to see it in action. It was so much shorter than before. We were all excited and nervous to see if this new simple format would yield any enrollments. Guess what? It did! The results were astonishing! The team began implementing this new format and duplication started happening all over the team. People felt empowered to do presentations now because they knew they could be successful, and they didn't have to be an expert. The power of a simple successful system can change your life and the lives of an entire team.

TIP: Having a simple system that your team follows is like having a magical advantage for their success and ability to duplicate.

Your focus.

What is your personal focus? Do you focus on helping your teammates get results on your products? Do you focus on building via Social Media? Do you focus on helping people rank advance? What exactly is your priority? For Bobby and I, we have always been single focused. Our focus is to find and build new leaders, and teach them leadership development in the Network Marketing profession. Bobby has been making this statement as long as I have been working with him, "Build leaders and teams will come". We pour all that we have into helping our team step into leadership. We create opportunities for them to step into more leadership roles as they build their business so their teams can grow. What we know is that the more leaders you have on your team, the more leaders they will find and/or develop. We have also focused on helping our team earn as much money as they can by teaching the compensation plan over and over. When you help more people on your team to earn higher incomes, it will create more stability in your business. What a wonderful thing to have duplicate through your organization. The healthiest teams are the teams where a lot of people are earning a LOT of money.

Here is the interesting thing about a strong team or strong company culture. Not everyone will fit. If someone's core values differ greatly, they will either evolve and change to fit into that culture or they will eventually leave. Speaking from years of personal experience, either outcome is welcome. Some people experience such incredible personal development as a result of being part of this profession, and being a part of a great team that they become deeply connected to its culture. Sometimes people are just not aligned and never will be, which can create a strenuous relationship instead of a healthy growing one. This can cause strife on the team as a whole. It is perfectly ok for you and for the team, that they leave. When your culture is strong, people will continue to stick around and plug in, even if their business is no longer growing. We have had this happen many times over the years. People had small businesses. They made $500 - $1000 a month and never grew past that, but they always showed up. They always volunteered. They were a staple and valued member of the team. Don't ever discount the people who continue to plug in and show up, even if they aren't your biggest team producers. Each person adds value to the team in their own special way.

" Build leaders; teams will come "

Social Media

Chapter 10

"We don't have a choice on whether we do social media. The question is how well we do it."
– Erik Qualman

When I began my Network Marketing career, there was no social media. There were no smartphones. Every home did not have a computer in it. Technology was just beginning to change and spread rapidly. In order to pursue building a business, just about every single interaction was face to face. If it wasn't face to face, it was a telephone conversation. This made it very important to carve out specific time to work your business. Network Marketing was done in the evening a vast majority of the time. Things didn't move as fast and it was harder to ignore people. Social media and advancing technology have completed transformed the landscape of the profession. There are now trainings and courses galore to teach you social media. You can pay big bucks to learn 'from the pros' how to maximize your business using social media. I don't claim to be a pro, but social media has been a major tool in building our business.

One thing you need to know as a Network Marketing professional is that you must stay current. You either evolve with technology and it's ever changing ways, or you will evaporate into the wind. I have enrolled and worked with FAR too many people that don't understand, use or even know about what is going on in the world of communication & technology, and how we use it to build our teams. Lucky for me, I have always been forced to stay up to date because of my three children. If I wanted to know what they were up to technologically, I had to learn it, use it and be a part of it too. If you are reading this and you were born before 1983, you are at risk of being left behind. If you did not adapt with technology as it was changing, you already are. OOPS! Don't freak out! All is not lost. You can easily begin to catch up. Information is more readily available now than any other time in history. To remain uninformed about something now is purely just a choice. YouTube and Google are amazing resources to learn from. I have a Masters degree from YouTube & Google University. I have learned so many things by searching for information on both of these platforms. I went through a crocheting phase, and watched many tutorials that helped me create some beautiful shawls and blankets. When I began podcasting, I knew nothing at all about how to do it. Everything I needed to know, I found on YouTube and Google. I have learned how to create excel documents, produce videos and so many other things because I took the time to search for it and learn it. If you are wanting to learn anything about a social media platform, all you need to do is use YouTube & Google.

TIP: Stay current with the ever changing landscape of technology, and you will always remain relevant in this profession.

Ok, let's talk Facebook. Facebook has dramatically changed the way we communicate with the world. First of all, we now have the ability to not only connect with, but be a part of people's lives all over the globe on a daily, hourly, and in real time basis. What used to be expensive, complicated and virtually just impossible, is now part of over 100 million people's daily lives. Yes 100+ million people are on FB! Before it became the marketing engine it is today, it was a simple way to connect with old friends, make new friends and see what was going on in people's daily lives. It gave people around the globe a way to feel connected to people we had lost contact with, and maybe would have never seen again. It has changed a lot over the last 5 years and will continue to change. There was a sweet spot for a few years where people were able to create a post and hundreds or even thousands of people would see the post. There were not the same algorithm limitations that are common today. This allowed the early adapters to Facebook the ability to have a massive social media reach. That massive reach allowed people in our profession to garner a lot of attention and grow their businesses in an entirely new way. This was the beginning of a new era in Network Marketing. Anyone could post their results and their passion because they were excited, and that would result in new connections, new customers and new business partners. This was the first time you could truly build your business, meet new people, connect with them via private message, and enroll them from your home without ever meeting them in person. People that were paying attention during that time built million-dollar organizations. As Facebook began to evolve, the FB admins got smarter and smarter about how people were using this platform for free to build massive incomes. It's obvious they wanted in on the action, so they began changing how and who saw our posts. They began adding new features and paid ads. With over 100+ million Facebook users, and many of them going on social media many times per day, it is an advertising gold mine. Today, two companies have the bulk of the entire advertising market share which is Google and Facebook who owns Instagram as well. ***Over 56.7% of ALL advertising dollars are spent on those two platforms alone.*** Not using social media for your Network Marketing business is just plain ignorant. I read in a recent business article that people are no longer buying from corporations; they are buying from people. This makes learning and utilizing social media as part of your business strategy a requirement.

While you may not be able to do what others did a few years ago, you can still use social media in powerful ways to build your business.

Social media for your business **is**:

- A way to achieve 10x your normal reach
- A way to show people every day who you are
- A way to create attraction marketing
- A way to connect and reconnect with people you know
- A communication tool
- A platform to create community
- A way to feature the benefits of your product/lifestyle/culture

Social Media for your business **is NOT**:

- A post and pray solution
- The only way to build your business
- A place to lose hours of your day scrolling
- A platform for drama or gossip

Let's dive in a bit. Facebook has a little older demographic. People on Facebook are spending a little more time reading posts. It is an incredible place to look for people who have been in your life and for them to look for you. Here are some tips. Make your profile public and your friends list private. If you want social media to benefit you, you need to be able to be seen by people.

Remember you are in control of what you post. If you don't want something posted for the world to see, don't post it! Start finding and friending people you know, people you worked with, people you went to school with, and anyone you can remember. When they accept your friend request, send them a private message and say hello. Begin to get acquainted with them again. The key to all social media platforms is consistency. You should be posting often, preferably at least once a day. Facebook likes it when you use the newest features they offer. The more you use those new features, the higher the reach of

> **" The key to all social media platforms is consistency "**

your post. Don't use Facebook to market your product like an ad. People always end up tuning ads out. Think of the billboards on the side of the road. We don't even see them anymore right? We skip through commercials altogether if we can, and we exit out of ads when they pop up on our devices. We subscribe to services like Netflix that don't even have commercials or ads. If your Facebook posts are mostly of you 'marketing,' people will begin to tune you out as well. Make sure to post things that will cause people to engage. They like seeing YOU and your life. They like what is true and authentic for you. People are starving for anything REAL, so give them real. Use pictures, videos and Facebook lives to show the world who you are, and why the heck they would want to be part of your tribe. You don't have to use those exact words. Just attract them to you with the person you are and are becoming. I have a quote by Jim Rohn that has been on my desk for 15 years. ***"Success is not to be pursued; it is to be attracted. You attract it by the person you become."*** Attraction marketing is all about attracting people to YOU using social media. Take some time and think about WHO you want to attract into your business. I have a list of the type of person and their character traits that I am looking for in new business partners.

- People with integrity
- People with passion
- Optimistic people
- Self starters
- Someone coachable
- Leaders
- Smart
- People who love people
- People with big dreams and vision
- People who are fun
- People with great energy
- People who value a healthy lifestyle
- People who want more
- People who are generous
- People who are loyal
- People who like to work hard

When I am posting on social media, I use that list to help me. What would a person with those qualities want to see or read on social media? What would attract them? You can be very specific with what you post when you know exactly who you're trying to attract. Sometimes this may mean that YOU need to make some changes, so that you can be the type of person who would attract the type of person on your list. That's ok, it is a great place to begin. It is good to use a variety of things in your posting to keep people interested. Don't just share other people's photos or incessantly post inspirational quotes. People will start tuning you out and scroll right past your posts.

Now let's talk about Instagram. Instagram has a younger demographic. They are less interested in reading and more interesting in scrolling. What gets their attention is the pictures you use. This platform is much more visually driven. Think of your Instagram page as your own personal magazine. What would you want on the pages? ***What would your ideal partner like to read in this magazine?*** This is great place to begin. There are a lot of hashtags, stories and direct messages. Hashtags are a big part of how to maximize Instagram. You can do some research to find out which hashtags you should use based on the type of followers you are trying to attract. You will need to learn how to create attractive looking images to post. If your images are eye catching enough, people will stay to read the caption. It is very important that you are interacting with people who comment on your posts and on other people posts as well.

Engagement is very important. Hashtags will help people find you, as well as help you find other people. Instagram stories are a great way to be more playful with your content, and not be as concerned with the esthetics of the images because they disappear in 24 hours, unless you make them a highlight. Highlights are a feature available on Facebook and Instagram, which allows you to keep what you post on your story long term. There are a number of features you can use to both find your perfect prospect and for them to find you. Again, I recommend spending some time learning about this platform and do your best to stay current on its features. Social media platforms change often so try to keep up!

TIP: Be yourself on social media. You will attract the right type of people for you to work with when they see who you are authentically.

I want you to know that learning how to maximize a few social media platforms is required in today's Network Marketing world. You need to have a presence. People want to see who you are and what you're about. When I meet someone new, I always ask them if they are on Facebook or Instagram, and if they are, I immediately add them to my friends list. When I have time, I scroll through their pages to see what type of a person they are. Social Media is a living resume for you to use to your advantage. Pay attention, the social media platforms are always in flux. They add features, take features away and make changes regularly. Do your best to keep up on the changes. You may just find another sweet spot, and be allowed to take advantage of something before it changes because trust me, at some point it will change. This goes for technology in general because it is constantly evolving. Stay updated on the new ways to communicate and share information with people. Years ago, Bobby and I would day dream about being able to project a meeting live to our entire team from the comfort of our own living room. Today that is a reality. We are able to communicate with anyone, anywhere in the world at any time, virtually for free. This still amazes me! However, if you don't know how, you will be left behind. Just the other day I did a group Facetime with someone who lives near me, and someone who lives in Australia at the same time. Crazy right? I also talk regularly with team in Germany from my home in Southern California. Technology has made the way we do business so much easier. I also use services like Fiverr to help me create logos, videos, and to help me with social media tasks, translations, creating subtitles for videos, video editing and SO much more! There is NOTHING we cannot do or create today because of technology. Again, remaining ignorant about something in the world today is just a choice. Information is readily available and much of it is free. There is no excuse for not knowing how.

While it is very important to stay as up to date as possible with social media and technology, it is also important to always bear in mind that social media may look completely different in 5 years. Some forecasters even believe that Gen Z will actually phase out social media. There is really no way of knowing, so you need to stay informed. You also need to continue to build the skills it takes to build your business outside of social media. I have shared many of them with you already in this book. Use social media and technology as one of your most important tools, but do not rely on it for your only method of building. I have met some of the most amazing people because of social media, and I used the other skills I have learned to turn those chance meetings into relationships. Some of those relationships have turned into very fruitful partnerships.

*" Use social media & technolo-
gy as one of your most important tools, but do not rely on it for
your only method of building "*

Building Up Your Armor

Chapter 11

"Hardships often prepare ordinary people for an extraordinary destiny." – C.S.Lewis

*A*t the beginning of this book I promised that I would give to you straight. Network Marketing is not for the faint of heart, that is for sure. It is a business of people, and people are imperfect. We all come with loads of baggage and we all make mistakes. Not everyone is going to see the twinkle in your eye and hear the passion in your voice, and just automatically be excited for you. Some will ignore it, some will criticize it and some will do their best to squash it. I wish more than anything that this wasn't true. I wish it wasn't true as part of this profession, and I really wish it wasn't a true part of human behavior. But it just is. Bobby has always told me that every Disney movie has a villain. This chapter is devoted to helping you to be prepared for some of the things that can happen and how to keep going.

Just know this. Every single person has their own journey. No two businesses are built the same with the exact
same circumstances. God created each of us with a fingerprint unique to us alone. Not another human being
on the planet will share the same fingerprint. By design
we are supposed to have a unique story and journey.
Comparing our results with someone else's will get us
nowhere fast. The only thing we should ever compare
is our level of activity - am I in as much activity as the
successful leader?

Right out of the gate I want you to become an expert at
NOT COMPARING. Theodore Roosevelt says, ***"Comparison is the thief of joy."*** Such a powerful and true
statement. It is so easy to look at someone else's success
or life and compare it to our own. They are building so
much faster, or they have this or that happening, and
I don't. They just got started and have already passed
me up. This type of thinking WILL NOT SERVE YOU,
and truth be told, it will destroy you. In this profession
we parade people across the stage and edify the leaders.
We have video clips, magazine articles and stories told
by the highest earners. Companies will give platforms to
the fastest movers, and all the while you will hear, do
not compare your journey with anyone else's. It is hard,
I know. It seems an impossible task sometimes right? I
can tell you, it is a necessary skill to develop. We build
our teams under the heading of 'duplicating', and yet we
are told not to compare. There is no way that anyone can
ever know the whole truth about anyone else's journey.

There are untold details that happen every day that you will never know about. There are things that either contributed to or detracted from the success that someone will have on this journey. There could have been years and years of preparation in the making to set someone up for big time success. And because there is no way we can ever know, we have no right to judge or compare. Our job is to be happy for others when they reach their goals. Our job is to stay in our own lane. In horse racing, horses are given blinders put on their heads that only allow the horses eyes to see directly in front of them. The jockeys and trainers know that if the horse is able to use his peripheral vision to see to the left and the right, it can easily throw the horse off course, distract him or even discourage him. So these blinders remove the horses ability to do anything but see right in front of him. I wish we could do that to ourselves and our team mates sometimes. Distraction is a powerful force used against us. ***Comparing ourselves to others is nothing more than a sad distraction.*** We were made to do what WE are supposed to do. We were designed with unique and special gifts that only we can use. We will have obstacles and trials specific to us, so that we may develop the specific skills needed to lead the ones we will be leading. There are people's lives that are meant to be changed because of your opportunity, and YOU are the only one who can do that for them. Stay laser focused and in your own lane. Your journey is for you and will inspire many people!

TIP: Take whatever steps necessary to keep yourself focused and in your own lane. Remove people from your social media if you need to, especially if it creates comparison & distraction.

One of the very first words my kids ever spoke to me when they were learning to talk was the word NO. With all the things we speak into and over our kids, we often use the word NO. We use it as a way to protect and teach them things. "NO, don't touch that it's hot. NO, don't run into the street. NO, don't pull your sisters hair." I suppose it shouldn't be such a surprise to us that NO is one of their first words. In Network Marketing the word NO becomes something that people are terrified to hear. The fear grows so big that people freeze up and stop talking to people altogether for fear of hearing NO.

If you decided you wanted to be an actor, you'd have to do many things to pursue it. You'd have to get some headshots and an agent, and then you must go out on as many auditions as possible. One thing that every actor, or would-be actor has ever said is that you have to get used to hearing the word NO. It is part of that world. You cannot fulfill your dream of being a movie star without paying your dues and hearing a lot of NO's. In Network Marketing you will hear NO more often that you hear yes that's for sure. I heard a top leader once say, "How would you like to be in a profession where you can fail 90 percent of the time and still become a millionaire"? The word NO is just that, a word. You don't need to add any emotion or subtitles to it.

One thing that we have done over the years on our teams to help reframe the fears that accompany that word, is make it a goal. Instead of avoiding the NO and being so hurt and impacted when you get one, we teach people to make it a goal every week to GET NO's. *In our accountability groups, one of the weekly goals is to get ten hard NO's*. It is harder than you think. Instead of focusing on the fact that someone isn't ready, you're now focused on how many people you can talk to, to reach your goal of ten NO's. This powerful exercise has helped to set people free from the fear surrounding that tiny little word. We even did a contest once and offered $1000 for the first person to get 200 NO's. Another thing you need to realize is this; NO is not an absolute. It just means not right now. You must remind yourself that it is about THEM (Your prospect) and not you. If they aren't ready, it is most likely a timing issue. The time for them to join you just isn't just yet. Now, there may be some skills you still need to develop, or some influence you need to gain before they will say yes, but no matter the reason a NO is always a NOT YET for me. Bobby told our current enroller NO for six years. The timing was never right. When you know what a NO means, you won't get derailed by them. When I was brand new to this profession, I was ignorance on fire! I wasn't sad or taken out by the NO's. I was surprised by them however and I remember thinking, "Man I thought you were smarter than that". It makes me laugh now! I had such a clear vision and felt so confident in my decision, that I couldn't believe it when someone else didn't see it. A wise man taught me, the yes's will build your business and the no's will build your character.

No = Timing isn't right

No = There is some trust or skill you still need to build

No = There are still questions they need answers to

NO does NOT mean you're a failure. Getting no's means you're out there talking to people and that is a good thing!

Let's talk about the naysayers, negative nellies and the crap talkers. No matter who you are, if you stand up for anything, decide to do anything that makes a difference, or pursue greatness at any level in your life, all the creepers come out of the woodworks. I cannot tell you why. Sometimes I think they are sent to help us get stronger, and sometimes it seems there only goal is to bring us down. Just like the story of crabs in a bucket. Have you heard it? If you put one live crab in a bucket, he will quickly and easily climb out, but if you have two or more in that same bucket, when one tries to climb out, one of the other crabs will pull him back down into the bucket giving him no chance for escape. Sadly people can be just like this.

TIP: Build yourself a support team; people who you can call when you need encouragement and will hold you accountable to your goals. Together you can help each other on the days you feel down.

First of all, what other people think of your dream, is none of your concern. Instead of wasting even one more second wondering why someone has said something mean, rude or less than encouraging you need to protect your dream. God gave it to YOU and it is not to be squandered or ignored. It is fragile and needs to be nurtured and protected. Hold tight to it! Protect it like you would a baby plant. Take care of it, feed it, give it what it needs to grow. Don't allow it to be neglected or it will die. If someone else doesn't understand, it's ok, they weren't meant too. Your dreams and goals are for you and your family. If people want to shoot you down for taking steps to improve your life and your future, then it certainly says much more about them than it does you.

I'd be lying to you if I told you hard times never come. They do, and sometimes they last a while. But trust me, it is only for a season. Guess what? Seasons change, so hold on and keep doing the activities you KNOW will grow your business. Stay focused on personal development and your day will come. In my career, there have been many hard seasons. Some of them felt like they would never end. Guess what, they always did, and every time I moved past the hardship of that moment, I had many new character traits and skills to take with me. The key is to make sure you are surrounded by people who are lifting you up. People who are going in the same direction as you, and people who believe in you. You will be a better leader for having gone through those hard times. You will gain belief and pride in knowing the kind of person you are is a person with GRIT.

TIP: Stay focused on consistently doing the activities you know are necessary to grow your business. It's like planting seeds in a garden. Plant, cultivate and one day you'll reap a beautiful harvest.

I want to share a story with you that I read years ago that really stuck with me. It was written by Don Mondell:

One day, the Devil laid out his gleaming, razor-edged tools upon a worn and ancient wooden table. He announced a 'fire' sale and carefully marked the price upon each tool:

ANGER: $100,
RESENTMENT: $400,
HATRED: $600, etc.

Each tool sold almost as quickly as it was placed upon the table. Toward the end of the day, a crooked old man in tattered rags approached. The man eyed the tools that remained, but was taken by a certain tool at the end of the table. The tool resembled the two long and bowed fangs of a viper. Its chrome-like pointy tusks caught the sun and sent flashes of blinding light everywhere. With one hand, the old man blocked his eyes from the glare and with the other, he reached for the tool. As he grabbed hold, the tool's steely needle tips nearly pierced his hand. This seemed to please the old man. He snatched up the tool and held it to his chest. With a glint in his eye, the man asked the Devil, *"How much for this one?"*

"I'm sorry, that tool isn't for sale," the Devil replied.

Without hesitation, the man said, *"But I'll pay double."*

The Devil narrowed his eyes and hissed, *"Sir, I've told you, that tool is not for sale, nor will I ever sell it. It is the most useful tool I own and without it, I wouldn't be half as effective in my work. With that tool alone, I can accomplish my every task. Now good day, sir."*

Dejected, the man looked once more at the shiny tool, then slowly placed it on the table. With almost a whisper, he said to the Devil, *"If I can't buy it, would you, at least tell me its name?"*

A slow and wicked grin grew across the Devil's face. *"Of course, old man, its name is ... Discouragement."*

Perplexed, the old man wondered out loud , *"Why is this tool so important to you?"*

The devil responded, *"It's more useful to me than any of the others. When I can't bring down my victims with the rest of my tools, I use discouragement, because so few people realize it belongs to me. Nothing paralyzes a person, nothing stops someone in their tracks like discouragement and hopelessness. Discouragement and hopelessness are no respecters of persons. They keep the un-*

employed unemployed. The homeless homeless. The sick sick. They can even draw the most powerful ministry to its knees. When overcome with discouragement and hopelessness, the person can't pray, they can't worship and they become a victim of their environment. Discouragement and hopelessness drains their victims of courage, vision, faith, expectation and the will to make a difference in the kingdom of God . If I can get you discouraged and hopeless, then I have successfully neutralized you. You are left with only enough energy to feel sorry for yourself."

Be very intentional about doing whatever it takes to keep your spirits up and your armor thick. This is my personal five-point checklist for not only building up my armor but keeping it strong.

1. Personal growth.

This is so incredibly important, not only for growing your Network Marketing business, but for also growing into a person that is bigger than the circumstances you encounter. That does not happen without digging in and doing the work to BE BETTER. For me personal growth has ALWAYS been spiritual growth. I have dug deep in my faith and used that as the catalyst for continuing to grow and stretch beyond what feels comfortable, intentionally seeking out my weak and blind spots, and working on being the best ME I can be.

2. Activity.

Staying in action will always keep your mind focused on the right things. I always look at my own calendar for the next 30 days, and if I am feeling discouraged, I work double time to fill my calendar with new appointments. Staying in the trenches is what will create momentum, and momentum means you will begin having progress. Nothing will fire you up more than seeing progress. That can only happen if you keep doing the activities required to build your business. Negativity and drama cannot co-exist with activity.

3. Vision.

The Bible says, "Without vision the people will perish". You need to know what you are working for. You have to cast that vision for yourself first. When that begins to get blurry or fade, you will be more susceptible to slowing down or losing your edge. Make sure to always have a crystal-clear vision of exactly where you are going, and keep it ever present. Look at it, think about it, visualize it, experience it in your mind. It is much harder to give in when you have SEEN and FELT your dream as a reality that is to come.

4. Goals.

Having specific measurable goals is imperative. You need an actual target to shoot for. Your subconscious mind will go to work FOR you when you give it a specific destination. Write down your goals and share them with someone who can help you stay on track and accountable. Then have a very specific and targeted action plan to help you reach small milestones along the way that will keep you on track for the big goal.

5. Support System.

This one may be the most important one. You need people. You need truth tellers. You need encouragers. You need people who can call out the greatness in you. You need mentors. You need accountability and prayer partners. These people are so vital to your success, it just can't be understated. Be very intentional about who you surround yourself with. These are the people who are on the front lines with you when you are facing challenges. You can, in turn, do that for others when they are in need. The power of your support system can be your strongest line of defense.

" Be very intentional about doing whatever it takes to keep your spirits up and your armor thick "

Replace Yourself
Chapter 12

*"Leaders don't create followers,
they create more leaders."*
– Tom Peters

*I*t is very important in the business world to keep
your competitive edge. If you have special skill sets
or information that gives you an advantage over others,
you can go far. In most cases, you're not giving away
this information to your competitors voluntarily. You do
everything you can to hold on to what makes you more
valuable than someone else. In the world outside of Network Marketing, you are very cognizant of people passing you up, or people taking a raise or promotion that
should have been yours.

That is NOT our world in the Network Marketing space.
That way of thinking will never allow your team to
grow and flourish. Network Marketing teams THRIVE
when there is a culture and environment that allows for

growth and development. There is no place for ego here. Ego will hinder not only YOUR growth, but the growth of your team. Network Marketing is the place we WANT to share every last bit of knowledge and skill we have developed with the people on our teams. Network Marketing is the place where we cheer if someone passes us up. Depending on the type of compensation plan your company has, you won't be worried about losing income if someone passes you in rank or earnings. We can freely and authentically mentor others in the hopes that they will be more successful than us. It is a beautiful thing.

No matter where YOU currently are with your leadership, you should always strive to have someone right on your hip growing with you. ***Your job is to look for, build up and support the emerging leaders that show up on your team.*** We want to help them to develop their skills and learn to do what WE are doing. This is the magical thing that sets Network Marketing apart from so many other professions. This is why simplicity is so important. Choose the few most important skills you need to learn and master them. Then begin training your partners to do the same thing. When I have been on a recruiting push, I enroll a group of new people that all get started in the same time period. My goal is to get them started properly and help them to begin developing their skills as quickly as possible. I want them to be proficient and self-sufficient in certain areas so they can begin to not only do some things without my assistance, but also so they can begin training their new people. This is a 'pay it forward' model. The faster I can create this chain reaction, the faster momentum will build for their team. I have found that setting a clear guideline and expectation is very helpful. Here is an example: I tell my newest partner to book 3 presentations right away so I can train them, and help them quickly begin earning in the compensation plan. I want them to win early in their journey. Here is how my system works:

1. I will present the entire first presentation as a training for them. They can watch how it is done, take notes, and grab their first few customers and business partners at the same time.

2. My new partner will help with the second presentation. They will step out of their comfort zone, share their story, and present part of the presentation. This allows them to begin to step into a leadership role and get their feet wet presenting.

3. For the third presentation, my new business partner takes the reigns. He/She will handle the entire presentation, and I will be there to support and help if they get stuck. By the time we get to the third presentation, they have had some of their own enrollments. They are building their confidence and belief, and they have earned in the compensation plan.

TIP: The faster you can get your new business partner into action, the faster they can begin developing the skills they need.

This is all by design. With them being aware that there is a limited amount of time I will do the presentation for them, they are paying closer attention so they can learn the ropes. They are forced into action even if they don't feel ready, which I have found is the best teacher. This frees me up to go do the same with my other new partners. I have found that when I stay with a new business partner too long, they begin to rely on me in unproductive ways, and think that they can't do what I do. ***This is NOT what we want people to feel***. We want them to believe that they CAN do what we do. It is my job to gently nudge them into that role. I continue to encourage them to take the next step. They don't need to know EVERYTHING yet. They just need to know the next step. I call this spoon feeding. All too often we try to give them so much information, and it can feel like they are trying to take a drink of water through a fire hose. When people feel overwhelmed or confused, the mind shuts down. We continue to empower and encourage our emerging leader to take the next step, and the next and the next.

I want to be clear about something that happens A LOT. What began as spoon feeding and gently nudging, can sometimes turn into dragging. We must always remember that this is a partnership. You cannot do everything for people all the time. You will end up enabling them instead of empowering them. Oops! You do not want to build a dependent, lazy team. ***You want to build an empowered team of go getters, independent self-starters and leaders.*** I have done both. I have learned the hard way that enabling people in business does not help them. It hinders both their growth and yours. On occasion I have broken my own rules about training and empowering and each time the same result occurred. The longer I spent training, the less confident my new partner became in their own skills. The result was that they never developed belief in themselves because I was always there. When I did try to break away and nudge them to take the lead, they were either mad, hurt or both. I was spending time with someone who had already been trained instead of training a brand-new person. As partners, your people should be meeting you halfway. If they fail to meet you halfway during the training process, and if they are unwilling to step up and participate with the actions you are suggesting, that is a clear indicator that this person is NOT ready to fully engage in the business yet. It is normal for them to feel fear and even be reluctant. But if they are unwilling, you have to be honest with yourself about where they are at on their journey. Love them, and allow them to remain a part time sharer of your products. Love them where they are!

TIP: Meet people where they are at, no matter where that is. If they are not ready to be fully engaged, love them and move on to someone who is willing to put in the time and effort.

I have learned that you match energy for energy in this business. When I find someone eager and excited who is not only willing but waiting for the next step, I will match their energy with as much training and support as they need. If a partner does not respond, if they are slow to take action, if they do not follow the system or coaching offered, I match their energy as well. They will not get the same type of coaching or attention from me. How do you know which is which? It is very easy to spot the emerging leaders from the rest. They show up on calls, they are engaged with social media pages, they are in contact with you a lot, they are asking questions, they show up to events, and they are doing three-way calls and presentations with you. *These people make themselves known with their actions*. Many people will say that they want to make it happen, but fewer will show you that they want to make it happen with their actions. Those few are the ones I am always on the lookout for and excited to work with.

My goal is always to find someone to replace me. I want

to develop a lot of leaders who develop a lot of leaders. You never want to have a team so dependent on YOU that they cannot stay in action unless you are guiding them. Your goal is to have so many leaders, that at any moment, you can be interchanged with any one of them. The way to develop these skills in your emerging leaders is to allow them to begin leading. Have them teach and train on calls or at events. Use them on three-way calls to share their story. Edify them and ask for their opinions.

> **" The way to develop these skills in your emerging leaders is to allow them to begin leading "**

Over the years I have asked things of my team that they felt they weren't ready for. I believed in them and their leadership, so I would encourage them to step out and try it anyway. Each time they were so proud of themselves and pleasantly surprised with the results. Recently I asked a newer team member to share her story at a local event. She would be standing up in from of approximately 200 people on a stage with 5 minutes to share how her results have turned into revenue. She was terrified when I asked her, but she courageously said yes anyway. I told her to practice her presentation and time herself so she would use her 5 minutes fully and not go over the allotted time. She did just that. On the day of the event, she looked amazing! She was very nervous and had never stood up in front of a large room like that before. I brought her up on the stage and handed her the microphone. Her hands were shaking but she absolutely ROCKED it! She was poised, articulate and touched everyone in the room with her five-minute testimony. After the event I chatted with her and she told me that she was so proud of herself, and she had an entirely new level of confidence and belief in herself.

Believe in people more than they believe in themselves. See more in people than they see in themselves. Then give them the chance to blow their own minds with what they can do! *Focus on finding leaders and pour into them to develop their leadership.* Then pass the torch to them, so they can pour into their emerging leaders.

Remember this ... you cannot take people to a place that you haven't been. Stay focused on your own personal progress. Are you still enrolling? Are you still bettering your skills? Are you becoming a better presenter? Are you rank advancing yourself? Are you rank advancing your team? Are you engaged? Are you plugged in? Are you showing up? This is a great little checklist for yourself. As you continue to lead yourself, you will naturally become better at leading others. When you are holding yourself accountable and to a higher standard, mentoring others becomes easier. You will know firsthand what it takes, what is working and what isn't, because you are doing it yourself.

Being a driver personality type, I like to do a lot of things myself. Often times I am impatient. I'd rather get something done myself with speed instead of taking the time to show someone else how to do it properly. This is a VERY bad habit to have in your Network Marketing business. "Wealth conceals itself to those unwilling to teach others, but wealth will reveal itself to those who take the time to teach others." I don't know whose quote that is, but it is SO true! Leaving your ego aside and taking the time to empower and teach others, will pay off in big ways.

" Wealth conceals itself to those unwilling to teach others, but reveals itself to those who take the time to teach others "

Goals

Chapter 13

"The greater danger for most of us isn't that our aim is too high and miss it, but that it is to low and we reach it." – Michelangelo

This book may be about how to build your Network Marketing empire, but this chapter can be applied to any part of your life. Surprisingly enough, most people don't set goals for themselves. Even more surprising is the fact that the few who actually do, have no idea about how to do it, measure it and hold themselves accountable to follow through and achieve those goals. A goal is not a wish that you 'put out into the universe' so it can be manifested. A goal is a specific and measurable achievement. Over the years I have found that lots of people say they have set goals for themselves, but there is absolutely no plan as to how to turn a goal into a reality. Want to know a little secret about me? I have rarely reached the goals I set for myself within the timeline I wanted to reach them. That's crazy isn't it? Does that seem sad or depressing to you? It doesn't to me. I like to set crazy big goals for myself! I like to think big! It is what motivates me to push myself and go hard. Here is a short list of how I set goals for myself.

TIP: Set goals for several areas of your life, not just your business life. Set relationship, physical and spiritual goals. Set fun and vacation goals for yourself and your family too.

I begin with the end goal in mind. I like to set 12 month goals for myself. Where do I want to be 12 months from today? I play a little game with myself. I think about what a reasonable goal would be, or something I feel very confident I can achieve. Then I go a little further. What would be really exciting to accomplish, but causes me to feel less confident in achieving? Then I ask myself, what would be an AMAZING goal to hit that feels out of reach and makes me feel flat out uncomfortable about achieving? That's the one I will land on! I will cement that as the goal I am working to accomplish. If you only choose goals that feel comfortable, how will you ever grow and stretch? You need to consistently keep yourself just outside of what feels safe and comfortable if you want to keep growing.

Next, break down your 12 month goal into quarterly

goals. This allows you to monitor your own progress. Once you have the big goal, you can set milestone goals based on shorter durations of time. After your quarterly goals are set, you can set goals for your first 30 days of action and activity. This first month can be broken down even further with weekly goals and day by day goals. Once you know what you want to accomplish, you can logically break down the specific activities, and the amount and intensity of those activities that you will need to do each day to reach those goals. I love to do this exercise with people on my team. I ask them a series of questions to help begin the goal setting process.

- What would you like to be earning in the next 12 months from your Network Marketing business? I encourage them to be realistic, but to also answer with what they really would want or need financially to have an impact on their lifestyle.

- How many hours are you willing to invest on a weekly basis toward achieving your goal? I need to know their commitment and willingness to work. This helps me to see exactly what amount of time they think they will need to invest.

- Are you committed to attending the company's big events this year? I will give them the dates and locations of these events. I want to see their level of commitment to immerse themselves in the business, and if they are willing to invest financially in it as well.

• Is there anything you need to give up right now in order to make room for your business? The funny thing about this question is that most people already know what needs to go. They already know what is not serving them or helping them to get closer to the life they want. Asking them to identify it is a powerful thing for them to say out loud. It will also help you as their coach/mentor to see what is taking up space and keeping them stuck.

TIP: Keep your goals in front of you so you cannot go one day without reading them.

If you have never done an exercise like this, ask someone in your upline (Your mentor or coach) to go through these questions with you. The next step is to write down all of the goals you have set including 12 months goals, quarterly, monthly, weekly and daily goals. You need to SEE them every day. You need to keep your goals in front of you. With measurable goals set with a date attached to it, you can easily self evaluate and decide if your current level of activity needs to change or be adjusted. This is a very powerful way for you to keep yourself accountable, and to help those you are coaching to stay accountable as well. Numbers are easy to track, and numbers make building your business quantifiable. This means you must also track your activities. If you are an unorganized person, I may have just lost you. But please stay with me here. If your goal is to financially set yourself free for life, you need to know what you did, how you did it, and how often you did it. This information will serve you well as you are training up new leaders. You cannot change what you do not measure. How will you ever know what is working and what is not if you never know what you did?

TIP: Keep track of the numbers in your business so you can make adjustments in your activity level. You can't change what you're not aware of. Track personal and team enrollments, volume in your business, personal and team rank advancements, and the number of presentations being given.

Once you have written down your goals, the next phase is telling someone else. There is a lot of data on reaching goals. It is said that you have more than an 78% better chance of reaching your goals if you write them down. If you tell someone else your goals, that percentage goes even higher. And if you are involved with others who help to keep you accountable, the percentage goes even higher yet. If you are going to go to the trouble of sitting down and setting goals, you may as well do everything you can to make them happen.

In the beginning of your journey you may be unfamiliar with practices like this. That's ok, your mentor/coach will help you. Setting financial goals in your Network Marketing business is partly done by knowing how your compensation plan works. You can use markers in your compensation plan to help with goal setting. Whatever you do, don't allow yourself to skip setting goals. Your brain is a powerful engine that never ever turns off. If you give it specific information, it logs that as truth. ***If you are not setting specific measurable goals, your brain has no target***. Your brain will go to work to help to accomplish your goals, but you need to give it a target to hit. Specific goals with dates attached allow your brain to have something very precise to work toward. A goal without a plan to reach it, is just a vague dream. It is ambiguous, or just words floating around with no meaning. I had a very bright woman on my team once who was fun, funny and full of energy. She wanted to double her income in the upcoming year. I loved hearing that goal. I encouraged her and told her she could do it! Next, I asked her what her plan was to reach that goal? She smiled and stared at me and said, "Well I don't have a plan, I just really want to double my income". The likelihood of her achieving that as a goal was very, very slim. In order to double her income, she would need a plan. People don't reach six and seven figure incomes in this profession on a wing and a prayer. That can only take you so far.

Some people don't like to set goals because they are afraid of failure. The thought of setting a goal and not reaching it brings up feelings of fear and inadequacy. So, they don't set any goals at all. The sad things is, this becomes a self-fulfilling prophecy for them. Their fears created the exact result they were fearfully trying to avoid. I understand that it can feel scary to set a goal, and it means you are now responsible for your actions. If you don't set a goal, then you won't be disappointed if you miss it. At least that is what people can think. However, this lack of intention most often leads to a lack of action. That most certainly will NOT get you closer to your goals.

"Lack of intention most often leads to a lack of action "

My advice to you is that you go BIG! Set some big goals for yourself, then devise a plan of action to get you closer each day to reaching that goal. Once a month, evaluate your progress. If you are not seeing the results you need in order to hit the goal, make adjustments, make changes, add intensity, increase your actions and re-evaluate again in 30 more days. This process will reshape your habits, not just in your business, but overall in your life. I am certain you have heard this quote, "***Shoot for the moon. Even if you miss, you'll land among the stars***". Les Brown said that, and he is right. Use goals as measuring sticks of activity and behavior. Not reaching a goal doesn't make you a loser or a failure in any way shape or form. The opposite is also true. NOT setting goals is a sure-fire way to LOSE big. Fear is a feeling, not a fact. Your life is in NOT in actual danger when you set lofty goals, so stop allowing fear to hold you back. Not reaching my goals has taught me the most. The more failures I have had, the closer I got to my dreams. You learn more about setting goals both by reaching them, and NOT reaching them. If you follow the process I have laid out and you miss your goal, guess what? You didn't die! Start again. Keep going. It is ok, and it is part of the process.

When you set big goals and you reach them, you create a confidence and belief inside of yourself that I can hardly describe. The feeling that is birthed inside of you when the moment arrives, and all the hours you've committed to, all the conversations you've had, all the miles you've driven, all the NO's you've taken, all of the hard parts … they all disappear. You know that if you can accomplish THIS , no matter how big or small the goal is, you can accomplish anything! I want you to know this. If you can make $200 in your business, you can make $2000, and if you can make $2000, you can make $4000, and if you can make $4000, you can make $10,000 and so much more. Want to know why? Because you are doing much more of the same daily mundane activities to get there. How fast or slow this happens totally depends on you; your sense of urgency, and your commitment to massive action.

When I have a big goal for myself, I know that the only way I will reach that goal is by helping people on my team reach their goals. That is one of the beautiful things about this business. It is just like Zig Ziglar says, "You can have everything in life you want, if you will just help enough other people get what they want". Go help people set goals and make their dreams come true, then go do it again, and again. Guess what, your dreams will come true in the process.

TIP: When your focus is on helping people on your team reach their goals, you will in-turn reach your own goals.

During a particular season of our business, I was in the grind. I was driving out of town several nights a week working with a fast-moving new group. The leader of this group was named Molly. She had a full-time job and worked her Network Marketing business in the tiny pockets of her life, and I mean tiny. This business model was such a gift for her. She could continue working her day job, and her team was growing because of the support and leadership on the team. About a year had gone by with this pattern of working her day job and building her dream in the tiny pockets of her life. She and I had driven about 165 miles round trip one night to work with some emerging leaders on her team. When we arrived at her house, we were tired but invigorated. We were working with excited people, who had big dreams! They were falling in love with the products, getting results and beginning to earn some money too. We were standing in Molly's driveway recapping the night. She had been involved with Network Marketing before and had worked very hard. She made some money but was never able to reach her goal of earning $10,000 per month. Her dream was to earn a six-figure income and see that elusive number of $10,000 per month. I knew how much she was earning every week, so I asked her "Molly, when was the last time you added up your weekly commissions?" She said, "I don't know, I have been so busy I haven't even thought about it". As we stood in the driveway, I asked her to pull up her commission reports on her phone, and I started adding them up for the last four weeks. Then I said "Molly, you earned over $11,000 in the last four weeks alone". We stood in the driveway and cried tears of joy! By helping as many people as we could, by staying consistent, by setting goals and making other people's goals our priority, she was able to reach her lifelong dream of a six-figure income in Network Marketing. I live for these moments!

Set goals for yourself, allow them to drive you and help you evolve. Set goals with the people on your team and stay focused on helping them become a reality. Do this again and again; set goals, evaluate, adjust. Set goals, evaluate, adjust. Keep going and stay consistent. Lives will be changed in big and small ways while you hit and miss goals. Before you know it, you'll be living your dreams.

" When you set big goals and you reach them, you create a confidence and belief inside of yourself that I can hardly describe "

Crash & Burn

Chapter 14

*"Only those who dare to fail
greatly can ever achieve greatly."
– Robert F. Kennedy*

Over and over in my career, I hear people talk about why they do not succeed, or why they cannot succeed. They use a multitude of excuses as to why they simply CAN'T make it happen. Bobby has always said this when it comes to excuses, "Any excuse will do, just pick one". All of the so-called reasons are exactly that... excuses, so it doesn't matter which one you use. Although there are many facets to building and growing a successful business in this profession, there is NO ONE who cannot learn and develop the skills required to do so. A large majority of people simply CHOOSE not to take the time to learn and develop those skills. Your personality, whether introverted or extroverted, is NOT a factor. Your background or upbringing, again not a factor. Your level of experience or even knowledge, also not a factor. There is truly only ONE thing that will determine your actual ability to build a massive team. Ready to know what it is? Your willingness to be a failure! Yep, I know. No one WANTS to be a failure. No one sets out to look stupid or embarrass themselves. We desire to be good at things and look like we know what we are doing. Winston Churchill said, "***Success is stumbling from failure to failure with no loss of enthusiasm.***"

We live in a world obsessed with perfection. We can filter our photos, touch up our faces, get plastic surgery and modify our bodies. We post images and stories on social media of the highlight reels of our lives. We glorify beauty and people whose lives look good. We put athletes and actors on a pedestal of almost immortal status. We watch TV shows about mansions, vacations and lifestyles, and we are truly mesmerized with the appearance of perfection. It's to the degree that unless we can do something and do it perfectly, many won't even try. This is a very unhealthy outlook in life, and it will KILL your chances for success in Network Marketing.

My first ever enroller in my Network Marketing career was a very cute, very crafty young woman. She could decorate and create beautiful things to look at. The company she was with used the party plan strategy. She hosted many in-home presentations. She would bring with her crates of decorations and boxes of props to use to create a beautiful display of products and snacks. It was so much fun! She did a very detailed and fun set up with a presentation that everyone loved! She would receive tons of accolades and compliments for her skills of creating such a fun party. People would say, "Oh you are so good at this, I had a such great time!" "Thank you for inviting me, I could NEVER do what you do!" (Insert sad dramatic music here.)

This is NOT what you want to hear as a leader in this profession. She was so good at the 'party', that people saw the set up and said "Wow, I could never do that. I don't have the tools or the skills". People didn't want to join her. They didn't want to have to do what she was doing to be successful. This can also happen when you have very skilled speakers and presenters. People LOVE to listen to them, and they enjoy the information the way it is delivered. They sit innocently listening to a fabulous presentation while telling themselves, "Wow, this is great, but I would never be able to do that." Outside of Network Marketing these excellent skills are very beneficial and can take you far. But in our world, perfection can sometimes be a curse.

TIP: Stop worrying about being perfect. It's a standard that no one can live up to. Just be yourself and show people anyone can build this business.

I am a really good communicator and always have been. I am not afraid to speak in front of people and I never seem to run out of things to say; just ask my very patient husband. I enjoy speaking, teaching and training others. We do a lot of trainings online in order to have high touch with our teams. A few years ago, I was hosting a Saturday morning training online. I had prepared slides and content and was ready to give the team some good information. Well, we all know that sometimes technology fails. Sure enough, on that day anything and everything that could go wrong did. And it ALL happened in succession. First, I lost my slides. Somehow, they disappeared from my screen. Next, my computer decided to restart due to an update, so I got kicked off my training. Luckily, I was also using a phone line in addition to my computer, so I was able to tell those who were listening on the phone line what was happening. I asked them to type into the chat what was happening to inform the rest of the team that I got kicked off. Once my computer started up again and I got the presentation back up and running, I finished the training. I made several jokes about not needing a lot of skills to build a business, and took the opportunity to make fun of myself and the calamity of events that occurred. I was sweating, and my heart was beating very fast, but I got through it.

Here is where the REAL lesson came. After that training, I received more text messages and emails than I ever had before. Each message was someone telling me how inspired they were by the training. WHAT?! This was clearly the worst one I had ever done! Why did this impact people so much? Each person told me that seeing all the issues that occurred, and watching everything fall apart and literally NOT work for me, inspired them in a BIG way. They saw that I didn't freak out or give up, but instead just kept going. This gave people a newfound confidence and level of belief. If SHE could do this business, and host a training where everything she did failed, but she kept going and did it anyway..... maybe I CAN make this happen too. It was the failure itself that inspired. ***When people see someone who isn't perfect or even great going for it, they don't look down on you, they are inspired by you.*** This is the lie of perfection. We fear being laughed at and talked about if we are not GREAT at something immediately. I was certain my training day disaster would live long in the Hall Of Shame and be something people talked about and scoffed at, but I was so WRONG! People were so happy to see the leader fail forward. They watched eagerly, waiting to see how I would handle it, and what would happen as everything was falling apart. My worst fears were being played out in real time. NOTHING was working! And yet, it was truly one of the most successful trainings I had ever hosted. I learned so much from this failure. I realized that in my imperfection, other people were empowered. If someone could fail in a big way, keep going and not let the failures take them out, anything was possible now. This was a huge turning point for me. I realized that allowing things to be imperfect actually benefited my team.

Giving other people permission to be a beginner and to learn as they go, is a very powerful gift. You can only get good at something when you practice. In Network Marketing your practice is how you begin building your team. You are NOT going to be great at first. You are not going to have ALL of the skills that you will need. If I'm being totally honest, you are probably going to flat out suck when you first get started. Doesn't it just fire you up to know that you can literally SUCK in the beginning,

> *" You can only get good at something when you practice "*

and you can still make money! How awesome is that?! The team that you are building and leading will learn SO much from your courage and perseverance to be bad before you get good. It takes time. Can you shorten the learning curve? Yes, you can do more presentations, talk to more people, do more three-way calls and draw out your compensation plan a LOT more. The more you do it, the better you'll get at it. You won't ever get good if you don't step up and JUST DO IT! Bobby has always said, "You can't be a permanent student." I am going to age myself a bit here but stay with me. When I was learning how to drive a car, I learned with a manual transmission, a stick shift. My poor Dad must of had whiplash as I jolted him around with every attempt to get my car moving forward. This new skill, moving both feet in opposite directions, and at the same time pushing the stick shift into the proper placement, and watching for traffic, being safe, following the laws... yikes! It wasn't pretty! There was nothing smooth about it. It was rough and jerky. What did my Dad do? He made me practice, and practice. Over and over I would stop the car and shift it into first gear. I would practice in parking lots, on the driveway, on side streets, and in as many places and ways I could to master the skill, and do it with ease. Over time, I could shift the car without concentrating. It became more natural and it wasn't as scary. After a few months it was smoother, and it became more automatic. I never thought about it, and I could now talk to people, listen to the radio, and do other things WHILE shifting the car. Practice! It is something you can't shortcut. You certainly have to put in the work.

TIP: Practice until it becomes automatic.

The same principles apply in your Network Marketing business. I am VERY good at presenting my business and products. Why? Because I have done it several hundred, if not several thousands of times. Trust me, I was NOT good at it when I first started. I was terrible actually, but I kept doing it. I built my business when I was VERY limited in my skills. Over time, I got a little better and I learned from my mistakes. I surrounded myself with people who were way better at it than me. I asked for feedback and worked at getting better. Malcom Gladwell says that it takes 10,000 hours of deliberate practice before you become a MASTER at a skill. I have accumulated well over 10,000 hours in my career so far, and I feel confident in my skills, but I will never stop practicing. I will never stop learning and working to improve.

Sadly, far too many people delay this process of deliberate practice for fear of not being good enough, or for fear of failing and looking stupid. I want to encourage you to pursue *fearless failure*. Go out and totally blow it! Go do a presentation and just completely SUCK at it! Get that part of your learning/training over with as fast as possible. Do it with passion and urgency! People will see what you're doing, and they will respond.

Here are two common responses to your terrible presenting skills:

1. Oh my gosh that was awful! I cannot believe how bad that was! I could do SO MUCH BETTER!

YES! This is a wonderful response. If the people you are speaking to or presenting for think these thoughts, you have won! They think they can do this better than you! You have eliminated the fear that they are not going to be good enough. That is a win!

2. Oh wow, that was really bad! Sheesh, if he/

she can do this, I can too.

YES! Again this is an excellent response for you! You WANT people to believe this business is something they can do.

Your lack of skill can be something that works in your favor. Stop being afraid to fail. Eloise Ristad said, "***When we give ourselves permission to fail, we at the same time give ourselves permission to excel.***"

Be deliberate about developing your skills. Go be bad, so you can get good. You must stick with a new skill long enough to make it automatic. Don't get caught up in the curse of perfectionism. There is no such thing as perfect anyway. Your ability to feel fear and do it anyway is what counts. Your willingness to walk toward failure is what will lead you to success. Allow yourself the time it takes to get better and allow others to watch. WHAT?! Yes, that is what I said. Your journey and actions will inspire your team to also take action. Watching you grow and develop skills gives them the confidence to do the same thing themselves. Your experience will give you the confidence to lead your team, to encourage them, to jump into action and develop their skills as well.

I want to add one last thing to this chapter. Being married to an introvert and giving birth to a few of them, I have seen how they respond to life. For Bobby, one of the worst experiences he can have, is one where he appears to be less than perfect. He avoids it at all costs. Starting conversations with people and speaking publicly are NOT naturally comfortable for him. The very things it takes to grow a massive business go against his nature and personal comfort levels. BUT, his desire to create a life of leverage and enjoy the residual life was bigger than his need to feel comfort. It was bigger than his need to look perfect all the time, although he usually still does, haha. He has developed incredible skills, and most people don't immediately think of him as the typical introverted personality type. He grew and stretched beyond his comfort zone to allow himself to master the skills he needed. Your personality is only a hindrance if you believe it is. Your background is only a negative if you believe it is. You are only going to be held back by invisible limitations that YOU and only you have set. They do not exist unless you give them the power to do so. I believe in you. Your family deserves it and you deserve it. Sprint fearlessly toward failure as if your life depended on it. Allow yourself to crash and burn. I promise, it won't kill you! It will burn off lies and limited thinking while birthing in you exactly what you need to get you to the next level.

" Pursue fearless failure "

Leadership
Chapter 15

"The task of a leader is to get their people from where they are to where they have not been."
– Henry Kissinger

T his may be the most important chapter in this book. It is so important that I feel like one chapter just cannot cover all of it, but I will do my best to give you the goods. *Everything rises and falls on leadership.* People chase after leadership, and more books have been written on leadership than any other topic. Leadership is so needed in every area of our lives, and it seems to be so lacking due to wild misconceptions. Leadership is not about your title. In my opinion it is all about your character. Leading in your Network Marketing business is not like being a manager at your job, or an owner of a business. Your team is a volunteer army. They actually choose to be led by you. There are as many styles of leadership as there are people in the world, and there is something you can learn from all types of leaders. Some things you learn and implement, and some things you learn and avoid.

Leaders use their words to awaken the unconscious, and they use their actions to inspire. A leader becomes a master at casting a vision. When you are prospecting someone, you are casting a vision for them of what is possible. You must paint a picture for them of a future that looks different, or better than the life they are currently living and sometimes complaining about. You paint a picture of how that dream can become a reality. You paint a picture of what it will take and how you will lead them to the promised land. As I use that specific vernacular, I am reminded of the story of Moses in the Bible. He was a very reluctant leader. He did not seek after it, but was chosen for it. God used him to lead millions of Israelites out of Egypt after hundreds of years of captivity and slavery, into a life of freedom from tyranny and servitude. I have studied this part of the Bible. As I have worked to become a better leader, I have had times where I felt that maybe I needed to stop. Maybe I should just sit back and take the easier road and stop trying to lead. But this story alone continues to inspire and teach me the value and importance of a heart led leader. As the story goes, Moses led millions of people out of Egypt on a journey to a land that was promised to them by God. This was a difficult journey. There were dangers behind and dangers ahead. There were people to care for, and problems to solve along the way. Without the leadership of ONE man, it was doomed to fall apart at any second. There was a time when Moses needed to leave the group to commune with and hear from the Lord. He went up to a mountain to pray and hear from God. Prior to him leaving, the Israelites were on track, moving forward, aligned in purpose and positive about the future. In the short time Moses was away, they lost focus, fell back into old patterns, longed to be back under Egyptian rule, and fearfully grumbled and complained about their newfound freedom. Upon his return to the tribe, it was his leadership alone that helped get everyone back on track by moving forward, and becoming a group that was serving one another again. ***People need good, heart-led leaders.*** Moses led, not out of selfish ambition, but from a calling to empower and serve others. Good leadership is so very important and needed. It is why I stay the course. I feel led to serve and empower as many others as I can.

I have heard many trainings from a variety of incredible leaders about 'leading from the front' or 'leading from the back'. It is my opinion that in this unique profession, we must do both simultaneously. Anything less will not allow for the type of leadership development that is possible. Leading from the front is all about you. You are a living breathing example of what your team is to replicate. Your actions show the way. You are walking the path for others to follow. They need only watch your actions and emulate them to find success. There is no need for you to TALK because your actions are not only proof, they are the tracks for your team to run on. I have already shared with you how incredibly important it is for your actions to be aligned with what you say. A BIG part of heart led leadership is character. To me it is the MAIN thing. When you are authentic as a person, so then will your leadership be. You are the person who always shows up to calls and events. You are the person

> **" There is no need for you to TALK because your actions aren't only proof, they're the tracks for your team to run on "**

who continues to bring in new people to the team, and then develop them into new emerging leaders. You are the one who talks about and promotes the contests and incentives. You are the most positive person on the team. You are recognizing and edifying other team members. You are continuing to earn ranks and promotions. Leading from the front means that the person you are, and the actions you take serve as the example for everyone else to follow.

Leading from the back is a little different. These leaders are doing their best to leave 'no man behind'. There is a strong emphasis on developing the emerging leaders on your team. You are focusing on working within your team to intentionally support and help people move up the ranks, earn commissions and rank advance. I have heard people say, "I haven't had time to work on my own business because I have been helping the team". This is a wrong way of thinking. When you serve your team in this way, you are working on your own business. There is so much value in helping the people on your team to move their business forward. The only way to have security on your team is by having a number of leaders who are all earning money. Leading from the back allows for mentoring, and skill development. You want to see your teams advancing their skills, and you are creating opportunities for them to do just that. ***You are gently nudging them in forward motion to stretch themselves to the next level.*** You are literally coaching people. This can mean asking team members to speak on calls, having them train on a subject they excel at, or asking them to speak in front of the room at trainings and events. It's also asking them to step up and take a more active leadership role at events, as well as hosting events. Over the years, I have found that most people just need a gentle push and some heartfelt encouragement to step into a bigger role. As a leader, your job is to believe more in people than they believe in themselves.

It seems to me that in most cases, a leader tends to gravitate more toward one or the other; leading from the front, or leading from the back. The best type of Network Marketing leadership does both. How do you balance it? It isn't really about balance. There will be times that you are enrolling a new group. Let's call it the new 'Class of (insert year)' that you'll be investing time with. Sometimes you'll have both going on at the same time, and you will feel busy. This is a very exciting thing when it happens! It means that you're beginning to have momentum. Do not allow an overwhelm to step in and slow you down. This is why having systems on your team is so wildly important. With good systems in place, you can easily handle both happening at once. A well-balanced leader is both a walking talking example, and great at developing new leaders. This combination will help you build a very solid team of leaders who build leaders, who build leaders. Your deepest desire is that this will replicate down into the depths of your team.

TIP: While balancing leading from the front and back, it is important to remember that 80% of your time should always be spent on working with NEW team. This includes prospecting, enrolling and training the newest team members.

As a leader, your job is to continue to grow. Craig Groeschel says, "When the leader gets better, the entire team gets better". I wholeheartedly believe this. You must continue to stretch and grow as a leader. Invest in your growth, read books, take courses and stay in groups of people that are better and smarter than you. Many times, in my career, I have asked other top leaders if I could pick their brains. I wanted to hear what they had done, what type of a person they are and what worked and what didn't work. Most people are open, and if you have the courage to ask, they will give you their time. ***You cannot expect your teams to value personal development if you don't value it.*** And remember, personal development will always be a key factor in raising your own level of influence. On our team, we have a monthly book club where the leaders will all read the same book at the same time. This is a fun way to open great discussions and bring new people into the conversation by asking them to share what they have learned from the book. We also do weekly and monthly challenges of which many are based in some area of personal development. We know the value of growing as a person and how that translates into growing as a leader. I can look back on my journey and see that I have grown and changed a lot over the years. I know that in order for me to continue to get results, I must continue to evolve. I know that I cannot be the same person this year if I expect to get different results. The same goes for you. So ... What will you do differently this year in order to grow yourself, so that you can get different results?

Leadership is about serving. Though most feel being the team leader is something glamorous, I want you to know that is not what it is about. The leader does more. The leader plans and prepares the calls. The leader plans and prepares events for the team. The leader spends hours putting things in place for their team, to allow for them to just show up and engage. The leader is the first to arrive and the last to leave. The leader gladly takes on tasks, so the team doesn't have to. Leaders spend the most money for team incentives, team dinners, recognition and rewards. It is these people who are willing to go the extra mile all the time, just because of who they are. They are not looking for kudos, accolades or recognition for it. They are serving their team out of love and the desire to see people reach their goals, have a great experience and have everything they need to do both. The leader often earns more than other people on the team, but servant leaders have truly earned it. ***There are many things done in private for the team that don't get talked about or mentioned, they just appear for the team.***

Leaders are the most consistent people on the team. They are people everyone can trust. They are the ones that people can count on to BE THERE. They are the ones people know they can call for questions. Leaders become such a staple and if they DON'T show up, people think something is wrong. It is definitely felt when their presence is missing.

Leaders are optimistic. They never ever stop casting a vision. They cast a vision for the future. They cast a vision for the company or team promotions. They cast a vision for earning freedom through income. They cast a vision for a better life through the products. They cast a vision for the calls. They cast a vision for events. They cast a vision for leading. They cast a vision for growth. They never ever stop painting beautiful word pictures for their teams. The energy of the leader raises the energy of the whole team. They are excited and excitable! They make everyone FEEL lit up and energized!

Leaders are truth tellers. Truth is one of my highest values. I cannot deal with lies or disingenuous people. As a leader I am not serving my team by not telling them the truth. Do not see this as permission to light someone up or rip into them. That is NOT what I am saying. What I am saying is that a leader is investing in your growth. If they see something that may need adjusting or improving, it is their responsibility to share that information with love and compassion. I am so invested in someone's growth and I care so much about seeing them reach their goals, that I cannot stand by and watch them do things or behave in ways that are not serving their goals. I will ask someone if I may coach them and if they say yes, I am truthful and compassionate. My goal is always for progress and growth, and to help someone get to the next level.

TIP: Every next level of your life will require a new version of you.

Leaders are fully immersed and engaged. They are always fully participating. They don't sit on the sidelines. They are down on the field, in action. Leaders lose credibility when they do not know what is going on and when they are not participating. You cannot tell your teams to show up on calls, and not be there yourself. As a leader you are the example of engagement and participation, in social media, on calls and at events. You are everywhere, all the time!

Leadership is not always pretty. Are you ready for this? I am going to share some of the harder parts that are not often talked about or shared in mixed company. However, I am all about being fully authentic, so I cannot write a chapter on leadership without including this too. Leaders take a stand. They put themselves in a position on the front lines. Leaders are the first ones to take on the arrows. What are the arrows you ask? The arrows are opinions, criticism, talking behind your back, people bad mouthing you, people trying to undermine you, people complaining about you and your leadership, people telling you that you aren't doing enough and people flat out being negative just because. I have yet to have met a true leader in this profession at any level who has not had to endure arrows. I was listening to a podcast recently and Lysa Terkeurst, a multiple best-selling author said, " If you are not taking arrows, then you are not leading." I am sad to say, this is part of the package. A long time ago, after attending my very first company convention, one of my team members (Who was someone that I considered a leader) asked me if she could talk with me. Without hesitation, I said of course. I was eager to talk and strategize. I was feeling the post-event high that comes after a remarkable few days at a big event. I was filled up and ready to take on the world. We had been in the company less than a year, had already achieved some incredible success, and I knew that after that event, she must have felt the same excitement and anticipation that I did. When we met, my eyes were literally sparkling with joy and vision. As we sat down,

> " **Leaders are the first ones to take on the arrows of negative opinions, criticism, talking behind your back, undermining & complaining** "

she began to cry. For the next hour, she berated me and complained about all the things I had NOT done for her, how I had wronged her, and how disappointed she was with me as a leader. (Insert popped balloon noise here) I wasn't only shocked, I was crushed! She and I had enrolled only a day apart. I was new to that company, just as she was. I was learning about everything in real time with her. By the time we reached this convention, Bobby and I had begun implementing systems for the team and were training on them regularly. However, when she and I got started, none of those things were in place yet. She passionately expressed her feelings to me about how I had not trained her properly, and how she had paid the price for my lack of knowledge. I felt that I needed to defend myself and explain to her that we had both started just one day apart, and that I was learning everything about the new company with her at the same time. I wanted to blast her back, but I didn't. I took a deep breath and conveyed my sincere apologies. I asked her if we could start again and promised to train her with the team systems we now had in place. I asked if she would forgive me.

This is just one example of the many times I have been blasted as a leader. I don't want this to discourage you, but if you want to have a massive business, you must be willing to take massive arrows sometimes. How have I survived? Thick skin, soft heart. It takes a VERY thick skin to be a leader. So many people feel it is their duty to share their opinions and dissatisfactions with you. They are all too eager to tell you the variety of ways you are doing things wrong. ***A thick skin is one in which you do not allow those opinions to create doubt for who you are and what you do***. A thick skin will protect you from harmful words and actions from others. Like water off of a duck's feathers, a thick skin allows words to be heard, then just fade away. Trust me this is a learned skill. It has taken me years to develop and truthfully, I am still developing it. Thick skin, soft heart. A soft heart is a little bit harder to develop. Your natural defense mechanisms will want to create bitterness and anger. It will want to defend you against the offenses thrown your way. A soft heart is all about grace. Offering forgiveness even if it isn't warranted. A soft heart is humble and tries to make amends with others who feel they have been wronged, even if you don't think they were wronged by you. A soft heart refuses to be angry, and instead offers compassion. A soft heart allows for others to make mistakes, be pardoned for them and joyfully move forward. Thick skin, soft heart. This skill will be tested again and again, but it will truly serve you well. Not just in your business but also in other areas of your life.

TIP: Learn to have a thick skin and never lose the ability to have a soft heart.

Black eyeliner. When I worked in the salon all those years ago, we used to say, "It was time to put on black eyeliner" whenever there was one of those days where we needed to have a little extra grit. There will be days when you need to put on black eyeliner in your business. You will need to dig deep for strength when someone has wronged you. You cannot build a giant business with a huge network of people and have zero conflicts arise. I think just knowing that this happens is so important. Many people are completely blindsided if something happens. The fact of the matter is, that it just will. Not if, but when. Sometimes people will blame you for their inability to grow personally. They will blame the leader if they cannot grow their business. They will blame the leader if things shift or change in their business. It is much easier to blame the leader than it is to look in the mirror and take responsibility for their own actions, or lack thereof. Sometimes they will lash out at the leader because of jealousy. Sometimes there will be no reason at all. People are all imperfect. We all make mistakes. We come with baggage and issues. We are in a business of growth and stretching, and progress can sometimes be painful. Sadly, when people are hurting, they take that hurt out on other people. Sometimes people will lash out at the leader and accuse them of issues that are really just a reflection of their own hang-ups. You will need to rise above all of it. You will need the support and encouragement of others who know you. *You will need to remind yourself who you would be if you weren't who you are*. It will pass. Be a beacon of forgiveness, strength and love. Don't become embittered and angry. It will not serve YOU even if it FEELS right in the moment! Keep going! Always remember, you were made to do hard things. Don't ever let someone else dim the light that shines through you.

Lastly, leadership is your ability to influence other people. Use your powers for good and not for evil. I have always believed that one person can change the world. Yes, that means you too. It starts with us. Who we are and how we impact the world around us. Yes, I know it is just a Network Marketing business, but really it is so much more. It is your chance to make a mark on this world through the lives of those you influence one person at a time. What do you want the world to look like? Be the change. Be the example. Begin the movement. Your impact may seem small at the beginning, but the ripple effect of the lives you touch can go on forever. Use it well. Serve others well. Lead well. Love a lot and don't forget to laugh.

" *Your impact may seem small at the beginning, but the ripple effect of the lives you touch can go on forever* "

Closing Thoughts

My goal in writing this book is to empower you with information and strategies that have helped Bobby and I build big teams. This profession is so powerful and can change just about every aspect of your life. The nature of this business allows you to impact many lives. As it evolves, and younger people are joining this amazing profession, I see less knowledge of what this really is and can be. Social media has taken over and so much emphasis has been put on teaching people how to build via those platforms. I wanted to leave behind a manual if you will, of what this journey has looked like for us. We have been around the profession long enough to have made it happen before technology had impacted it so deeply. I still believe the tried and true foundation of this business will always be relationships. I believe one of the big things that attracts people to the profession is financial freedom. Many feel uncomfortable talking about that part. My question for you is this, "What problem(s) are you currently facing that would completely dissolve into thin air, with MORE money? It really is ok for it to be about the money. Let us never forget the power of offering people a way to build a financial legacy for themselves. This is attractive to men and women of all ages, groups and demographics.

I wanted to share the things I have learned along the way, both from my amazing mentor Bobby and from real world circumstances. I wanted to offer another tool for you to utilize. My hope is that this book gets USED, highlighted and pages folded down. I hope you will share it with your teams. I hope you will send me testimonials of the massive organizations you have built and your stories of freedom. I want nothing more than to continue to highlight and elevate this profession that I love so much. ***It is ALL of our responsibilities to keep it alive, and to make it a place of integrity and hope.*** We are all in this together, no matter what company you're with, no matter what country you live in, and we need to lift each other up. We need to hold each other accountable and to a higher standard. We need to keep the legacy alive! The legacy of hope, freedom and a life by design.

Thank you for caring enough about your future to invest in reading this book. Go help as many other people as you can, as fast as you can, and live YOUR dream!

Wishing you massive success!

xoxo

Michelle

"This profession is so powerful - it changes every aspect of your life and allows you to impact many lives."
– Michelle Schaffer

BOOK MICHELLE FOR YOUR NEXT EVENT:

www.michelleschaffer.com

Michelle's a sought-after sales trainer in corporate America. Her experience, powerful stories & humor entertain & equip aspiring high earners! You'll want your team around her energy, gaining her "grit" mentality, learning how to take massive, consistent action and embracing coachability.

You'll learn things like raising your influence, using social media effectively, disciplining yourself in measuring what really matters and the emotional intelligence you'll need to build strong relationships. No B.S. The best part - **Michelle's DONE IT!** Let her help **fast track your team's success!**